READY, SET, GO!

PLAYBOOK FOR CAMPAIGNS, CANDIDATES, AND CAUSES

Kacey Carpenter

Carpenter Publishing

Copyright © 2023 by Kacey Carpenter

All rights reserved. No part of this book may be reproduced in any manner whatsoever without written permission except in the case of brief quotations embodied in critical articles and reviews.

ISBN: 979-8-9897006-0-8 (Paperback)
ISBN: 979-8-9897006-1-5 (Ebook)

First Printing, 2023

READY, SET, GO!

DEDICATION

This book is gratefully dedicated to all the progressive change-makers. Thank you to all the people who support campaigns, candidates, and causes for your commitment, purpose, and service to a future to believe in for all.

Contents

Dedication   v

Step One: READY

One
Find Your Purpose   3

Two
Get Involved   25

Three
Create Your Plan   53

Step Two: SET

Four
Form Your Organization   81

Five
Run for Office   110

Six
Craft Your Message   140

Step Three: GO!

Seven
Organize a Movement   163

Contents

Eight
Get Out the Vote — 199

Nine
Count Every Vote — 229

Resources — 253
Acknowledgements — 261
About The Author — 262

Step One: READY

All we are saying is give peace a chance.

—*John Lennon*

John Lennon, a legendary musician, peace activist, and dreamer, was a passionate advocate for peace, prosperity, and love. Lennon envisaged a harmonious world without divisions or conflict, where people live united, without borders, religions, or possessions. His dream was of a world rooted in love, acceptance, and understanding. The lyrics of "Imagine" continue to inspire those building a movement for peace, prosperity, and love. Lennon's enduring legacy stands as a beacon of hope and a call to action for dreamers everywhere.

Welcome to **READY, SET, GO!** your comprehensive guide to making a difference in your community. Whether you are just starting out or already engaged in a campaign, this book is your go-to guide for community involvement. It echoes the inspiring words of John Lennon and many others who share a vision for a better world. It provides a roadmap for getting involved and making a difference in your community with best practices, success stories from around the country, lessons learned from many campaigns, candidates, and causes, and steps to get started.

This book is designed for everyone, from students to retirees, beginners to seasoned experts. It offers a step-by-step journey into campaigning, running for office, or championing a cause. However, it also serves as a reference for those seeking specific insights. The playbook is enriched with resources and references, providing additional layers of knowledge and expertise. It encourages thoughtful reflection and engagement, making it a valuable tool for your group or grassroots organization. The exercises and questions within the book are designed to foster continuous learning and growth.

It is a call to action for all change-makers. It equips you with the tools to kickstart and maintain initiatives of any scale, whether they last days or years. Your path to making a difference, locally, nationally, or globally, starts with three simple steps: ready, set, go!

1. **READY:** The first step is to discover your purpose and the change you want to effect. Once clear on your purpose, connect with others who share it, such as family, friends, neighbors, and colleagues. Research your community to find stakeholders, understand their needs, and build alliances. Create your plan with your goals, a strategy, and a roadmap to achieve them. Once your draft is ready, review it with your network, listen to their feedback, and encourage their participation.
2. **SET:** This next step is all about preparation. With a clear purpose and plan in hand, you are ready to form your organization, decide to run for office, and craft your message. This step lays the foundation for your campaign, candidate, or cause.
3. **GO!** This step is the action phase when you bring your plan to life, engage your base, communicate your message, and work relentlessly towards your campaign, candidate, or cause's goals.

One

Find Your Purpose

Look, it's not about me, it's about us, and when we stand together, we can do anything.

—Bernie Sanders

Bernie Sanders, the senior U.S. Senator from Vermont, and a recent candidate for President of the United States, inspired me to find my purpose. In December 2015, I attended Bernie's campaign rally in Reno, Nevada. His speech moved me, along with more than one thousand chanting, cheering, and clapping supporters in the audience. He directly asked each of us to volunteer our time, vote for our values, and believe that our voices matter and that *"when we stand together, we can do anything."*

Bernie spoke with passion about the important issues, to think big about what is possible, and to believe in a future for all. At that moment, I understood my purpose and committed to focusing my energy, enthusiasm, talents, and time to volunteer for the campaign that would grow into a movement. That day changed my life and soon I would travel around the country as a volunteer on my journey with Bernie.

In this chapter, you will start your journey to discover your purpose. You will explore what drives you, the causes that matter the most to you, and how to use your passion, unique talents, and superpowers to address important community needs. You will learn how to:

- **Find your passion:** Figure out what excites you and fuels your sense of purpose.
- **Uncover your skills:** Find out what you are good at and how you can use them to help others.
- **Do what you enjoy for good:** Identify what brings you joy, learn how to do it well, and help others.
- **Define your mission:** Explore different causes and decide if you want to focus on one or if you are interested in several.
- **Seek satisfaction:** Pinpoint what makes you happy to maintain balance and avoid burnout.
- **Write your purpose statement:** Create a statement that combines your passions, skills, mission, and rewards. This will help guide your next steps and connect with others who share your purpose.
- **Draw inspiration:** Learn from profiles of successful people who have followed their purpose. These stories will inspire and guide you on your journey.

By the end of this chapter, you will have a clear understanding of your purpose and some ideas for your campaign, candidate, or cause.

What Is Your Purpose?

You are reading this book because you care about making a difference in your community. Like Lao Tzu, a Chinese philosopher said,

"*A journey of a thousand miles must begin with a single step,*" and your first step is to figure out what truly ignites your purpose.

What issues do you think need attention? Maybe it is something local in your neighborhood - like making sure kids have safe routes to school, clean air to breathe, clean water to drink, or affordable housing for everyone.

Every day we read negative stories in the newspapers, and watch cable network commentators relentlessly feature reports concerning the many problems in our communities, country, and the world, and we see so many problems at home in our communities. It can feel overwhelming and exhausting. But there are people out there who are stepping up, making a difference in their communities, organizing for change, running for local office, and taking the initiative to change the world.

Can you spare 30 minutes a day? Use this time to discover your purpose. Identify what matters to you, what stirs your passion, and what issues in your world motivate you to act. Reflect on these in a quiet spot, jotting down your thoughts or recording them. Observe your surroundings - your neighborhood, workplace, or school - and consider what they need.

Start a journal to record your ideas. Celebrate the time you invest in this daily routine, which will soon become a habit. As your focus sharpens, you may find yourself dedicating more time to this exercise. If you prefer company, invite a friend or colleague for a coffee or lunch, or join a club. Find the approach that suits you best.

Ikigai: An Exercise to Discover Your Life Purpose

Many of us are not able to find purpose and struggle to find the balance in our lives and the time and energy for purpose, satisfaction, and joy.

Ikigai, a Japanese philosophy that combines the terms *"ikiru"* (life) and *"gai"* (reason), refers to your life purpose or reason for being. This concept is rooted in Okinawa, Japan, an area known for the longevity, happiness, and sense of purpose of the people living in this community. Discovering, pursuing, and nurturing your Ikigai or purpose brings meaning to your life. Having a purpose in your life can help you achieve a state of flow in everything you do, leading to happiness and improved health.

The practice of Ikigai involves finding a balance between your passions, skills and talents, mission, and rewards. In other words, it is about aligning what you love, what you are good at, what the world needs, and what rewards you. You can practice Ikigai by asking these four questions:

1. **Passion:** What do you love?
2. **Skills and talents:** What do you do best?
3. **Mission:** What does the world need from you?
4. **Reward:** What do you need to find satisfaction?

Passion: What Do You Love?

By reflecting on these questions, you will gain a deeper understanding of your life's purpose and find fulfillment in your daily activities. Take a moment to figure out what you love to do, your passion. Starting with what you enjoy and are truly passionate about can help maintain your energy and commitment in the long run. Some of our most significant accomplishments take longer than we expect, so focus on what brings you the most joy. When you dedicate your time to what you love, you will find the motivation to do meaningful work for your campaign, candidate, or cause.

 Tip

If you are finding it difficult to identify your top three passions, here are some strategies to help you:

1. **Review your daily routine:** What activities do you look forward to each day?

2. **Consider your learning interests:** What topics do you enjoy learning about in your free time?

3. **Observe your reading preferences:** What articles or books do you find interesting?

4. **Reflect on your hobbies:** What hobbies do you love to engage in during your free time?

5. **Check your social media:** Which social media content do you find inspiring and consistently engage with?

Need help? Here's a list of ideas:

- **Animal care:** Giving love and a safe home to furry friends. You enjoy their company and build a bond of trust and love.
- **Art:** Creating and expressing new ideas and emotions through a chosen medium. It involves capturing the beauty in the world, communicating with others, and challenging perceptions.
- **Coaching:** Guiding people or teams to be the best they can be. You help them set goals, support hard work during practice, and then celebrate their achievements and learn from mistakes.
- **Counseling:** Helping others navigate their mental and emotional challenges. This involves providing a safe space for people to explore their feelings and thoughts and offering support and guidance.
- **Gardening:** Nurturing plants and creating beautiful landscapes. It involves enjoying the tranquility that comes from spending time outside, connecting with nature, and caring for the environment.
- **Music:** Expressing emotions and stories through melodies and rhythms. It involves bringing joy to others through musical performance and connecting with other musicians and listeners.
- **Photography:** Capturing the world through a lens. It involves preserving moments in time and telling stories

through images. It involves seeing beauty in ordinary things and sharing unique perspectives.
- **Reading:** Diving into different worlds through words. It involves gaining knowledge, understanding diverse perspectives, expanding one's imagination, and enriching one's vocabulary through literature.
- **Researching:** Seeking knowledge and solving complex problems. It is like being a detective in the world of knowledge. You dive deep into a topic, uncover new facts, and solve tricky problems.
- **Serving others:** Making the world a better place, one person at a time. You find joy in helping others and contributing to their well-being.
- **Teaching:** Sharing knowledge and inspiring curiosity. You help students learn, grow, and succeed.
- **Volunteering:** Giving time and effort to help others or contribute to a cause. You help others or support a cause close to your heart.

Passion: What Do You Love?

Now it is your turn. List your top three passions here.

1.

2.

3.

Skills: What Do You Do Best?

Make a list of your skills and talents, the things you are good at. This includes both your soft skills (like communication or teamwork) and hard skills (like coding or writing). Think about the tasks or roles that you find easy, or that others have complimented you on. Now is not the time to be humble. It is okay to take pride in what you do best. Here is a helpful tip to get started.

 Tip

Discovering your skills, talents, and superpowers involves understanding what you do best. Your gifts, skills, and talents are not always visible, but they can significantly enhance the effectiveness and harmony within a volunteer organization. Here are some strategies to help you identify your top three skills or talents.

1. **Reflect on your career and job skills:** Consider the skills you have developed in your professional life. These could be technical skills related to your job or transferable skills like problem-solving or communication.

2. **Consider your educational experiences:** Think about the subjects or areas where you excelled in the classroom. This could provide insights into your natural talents.

3. **Listen to others:** Often, people around you can provide valuable insights into your strengths. Think about the times when people have complimented you or asked for your help because they trust your abilities. These are clues to what you are good at.

4. **Consider what you enjoy and find easy to do:** We often excel at things we love because we naturally spend more time on them. So, do not overlook activities that you find effortless or that you lose track of time while doing.

Need help? Here's a list of ideas:

- **Campaign management**: Strategic planning and coordination, managing a campaign.
- **Cartooning:** Creating humorous and thought-provoking cartoons.
- **Communication**: Clearly expressing thoughts and ideas, and effectively receiving information from others.
- **Critical thinking**: Objectively analyzing and evaluating issues to form a judgment.
- **Data analysis**: Working with numbers spotting trends and informing stories for campaigns, candidates, and causes.
- **Filmmaking:** Telling stories through the medium of film and creating cinematic experiences.
- **Fundraising**: Persuading people to financially support a campaign, candidate, or cause.
- **Inventing:** Solving complex problems and pushing the boundaries of what is possible.
- **Leadership**: Being a guiding light for your team. You inspire them towards a shared goal, motivate them, empower them, and guide them on their journey.
- **Public speaking**: Being comfortable speaking in front of large groups.

- **Research**: Gathering, analyzing, and interpreting information effectively.
- **Strategic planning**: Developing effective strategies and plans.
- **Writing**: Crafting compelling narratives, content, and stories.

Skills and Talents: What Do You Do Best?

Now it is your turn. List your top three skills and talents here.

1.

2.

3.

Mission: What Does the World Need?

Think about the mark you want to leave on the world - the changes that matter to you. This is your mission, your driving force. To discover your mission, ask yourself: Who are the people you are passionate about helping? What challenges are they facing? Your mission is all about using your special skills to make a difference in the world.

 Tip

Finding your mission is important to focus your purpose on the most important issues in your community, our country, or the world. If you are struggling to pinpoint what matters most to you, here are some strategies to help you align your heart and your mind:

1. **Name your emotions:** Start by reflecting on the headlines or stories that stir strong emotions within you. These could be issues tied to social justice, saving the environment, education, health, or any other challenge. How you feel about these issues can show what truly matters to you.

2. **Reflect on your contributions:** Think about the causes and organizations you are already supporting. This can give you a clue about where your mission lies.

3. **Analyze your character:** Think about your favorite movie and the character you identify with the most. Analyzing why you connect with that character can provide insights into the types of missions that resonate with you.

4. **Match your mission with needs:** Reflect on what your community, country, and the world need today. Try to find a match between these needs and your desired life purpose. This could be anything from mentoring young people in your community to contributing to global initiatives.

Need help? Here's a list of ideas:

- **Aging and healthcare:** Supporting the well-being and dignity of older adults and ensuring access to quality and affordable healthcare for all.
- **Animal welfare:** Supporting pet adoption initiatives and animal rights organizations.
- **Anti-racism and discrimination**: Standing up against systemic racism and discrimination and pushing for equal opportunities for everyone.
- **Civil rights**: Ensuring and protecting people's rights, including reproductive freedom and LGBTQ+ rights, because you believe these are fundamental human rights.
- **Climate change and environmental justice**: Advocating for policies to fight climate change and promote sustainable practices. Show up for communities that are disproportionately affected by environmental hazards.
- **Community safety and wellness**: Working towards creating safe routes to school, controlling guns, promoting organic gardens in public spaces, and ensuring stable housing and high-quality childcare.
- **Criminal justice reform**: Reforming criminal justice and prisons to end mass incarceration and ensure policing is protective for all people.
- **Economic inequality**: Creating living wage jobs and fairly sharing the burdens of government through innovations in land ownership, workers' conditions, banking, regulation, and taxes.
- **Education reform**: Promoting, expanding, and improving education. Ensuring access to high-quality, affordable education from preschool through college. Tackling issues like unfair student loans, low pay, and understaffed facilities, and advocating for fair wages for teachers.

- **Food security and anti-poverty**: Helping people get the food they need by supporting food banks, community gardens, and affordable housing initiatives.
- **Freedom of speech, press, protest**: Protecting our democratic rights to speak freely, have a free press, and the right to protest.
- **Immigration reform**: Advocating for fair immigration policies that provide a path to citizenship for undocumented immigrants.

These causes are crucial, each presenting a significant opportunity for grassroots organizers to make a real impact. Despite the challenges, maintaining optimism is key. Throughout history, people have successfully achieved incredible feats, such as landing on the moon and building the global Internet, proving that you can create change too. By uniting diverse groups, you can amplify your impact. Climate change affects our daily lives and economy, while inequalities cut across demographics, ages, and geographies. It's not just about identifying problems; it's about being the driving force behind transformative change. You have the power to make a difference.

Mission: What Does the World Need?

Now it is your turn. List your top three missions here.

1.

2.

3.

Reward: What Do You Need to Find Satisfaction?

The final step in defining your Ikigai is to match your needs for reward. While you may find your purpose aligns with your profession, for many, the rewards extend beyond monetary compensation. It is crucial to identify what satisfies you to maintain balance and prevent burnout. Understanding this is crucial to align your life with your Ikigai.

 Tip

> Here are some strategies to help you understand your personal needs for reward and recognition:
>
> 1. **Reflect:** Take some time for self-reflection to think about what makes you happy and fulfilled. This could be the joy of helping others, learning new things, overcoming challenges, or achieving a personal goal.
>
> 2. **Identify your values:** Understanding your values is a big part of what drives your satisfaction. These are the things that make you feel good about what you are doing.
>
> 3. **Consider past experiences:** Think about times when you felt most satisfied and fulfilled. What were you doing? Who were you helping? What problem were you solving? This can give you clues about what rewards are most meaningful to you.

4. **Balance:** Ensure there is a balance between giving and receiving. While it is important to contribute to your community or cause, it is equally important to take care of your own needs and well-being to avoid burnout.

5. **Seek feedback:** Do not hesitate to ask for feedback from those who know you well. They can provide valuable insights into your strengths and the impact of your contributions.

Need help? Here are some ideas for possible rewards:

- **Compensation:** Receiving a salary or wage for your time and contributions.
- **Creative expression:** Expressing yourself creatively through your work.
- **Experience and Networking**: Gaining experience and building valuable relationships and connections in your community or through volunteering for a cause you care about.
- **Flexible schedule:** Setting your hours or working remotely.
- **Making a difference:** Contributing to a cause or mission that you care about.
- **Mental acuity:** Keeping your mind sharp by challenging yourself intellectually.
- **Personal fulfillment:** Doing something you love or are passionate about.
- **Physical health:** Improving your health and fitness by doing physical work, such as canvassing and knocking on doors for your candidate.

- **Recognition:** Being acknowledged for your contributions.
- **Skill development:** Learning and growing through your work.
- **Travel opportunities:** Traveling, either domestically or internationally, for your work.
- **Work-life balance:** Balancing your work commitments with your personal life.

Reward: What Do You Need to Find Satisfaction?

Now it is your turn. List your top three rewards here.

1.

2.

3.

Your Purpose Statement

After identifying your passions, skills, mission, and rewards, you can craft your Ikigai statement. This concise summary of your purpose will guide your next steps on your journey. Here are a few examples to consider:

- Follow your passion for gardening and cooking and use your skills in teaching and library management to establish a seed library. This supports your mission to contribute to a healthier and more sustainable planet. The rewards are personal fulfillment from doing what you love, recognition for your contributions, and the opportunity to help others learn.

- Embrace your mission to contribute to a healthier and more compassionate world for our furry friends. Utilize your Red Cross Cat and Dog First Aid skills and offer pet-sitting services in people's homes. The rewards you seek include the physical health benefits of walking dogs, the travel opportunities that come with pet sitting, and the personal satisfaction of supporting animal welfare initiatives and animal rights organizations.
- Cultivate your passion for volunteering in your community, with a focus on anti-poverty. Utilize your talents and skills as an author and speaker, dedicated volunteer, and efficient organizer. Your mission is to build a world where hunger is a thing of the past and everyone has access to nutritious food and healthcare. It is a vision of a healthier, more equitable world. You organize fruit gleaning, source, and distribute produce to community food pantries, and advise aging women on healthcare planning options. The rewards you seek are recognition for your efforts, appreciation from those you help, and the friendship of others who share the same values.
- Perform uplifting songs with passion at meetings and community events, serving others through music. Share your gifts, skills, and talents in teaching, organizing, and volunteering for your local non-profit group. This community group is all about supporting campaigns, candidates, and causes that cover a wide range of important issues, from fighting for climate justice to pushing for education and healthcare reform. Your mission is to help create a world where these issues are tackled head-on, and together we are making strides toward equality and justice. The reward you seek is the fulfillment that comes from making a difference in causes that you deeply care about.

- Unleash your passion for making a positive change in your community and country, despite the many challenges we face. Use your leadership and public speaking skills to run for office, with a mission to serve, lead, and bring about change. The reward you are after is the satisfaction that comes from serving your community and seeing the positive effects of your hard work.

★Success Story Profile: Danny Glover★

Danny Glover, actor, director, producer, and political activist started his journey towards a life of purpose while studying at San Francisco State University (SFSU). As part of the Black Students' Union, he took part in the longest student walkout in U.S. history, pushing for the creation of a Department of Black Studies. This early experience in activism laid the foundation for his lifelong commitment to social justice.

Glover's activism extends beyond academia. He has been a vocal advocate for various causes, including labor rights, healthcare reform, and racial equality. His support for the United Farm Workers and service unions exemplifies his dedication to labor rights. Glover's activism is not limited to domestic issues; he was arrested outside the Sudanese Embassy during a protest over Sudan's humanitarian crisis in Darfur. His dedication to his causes is clear in his relentless advocacy and his use of his platform to bring about change.

In politics, Glover has actively supported several presidential candidates. He endorsed Bernie Sanders for president in both 2016 and 2020 and spoke at several grassroots events for the candidate. Glover's commitment to these candidates and their platforms demonstrates his alignment with their missions and his reward for contributing to their campaigns.

★Success Story Profile: Greta Thunberg★

Greta Thunberg, an autistic climate justice activist, was born on January 3, 2003, in Stockholm, Sweden, at 375 ppm. She is a globally recognized environmental activist who founded the Fridays for Future movement in 2018. Her journey began in childhood when she learned about climate change at the age of eight. This sparked a personal transformation, leading her to become a vegetarian and refuse air travel due to their significant contributions to global warming.

Diagnosed with Asperger syndrome, now considered an autism spectrum disorder (ASD), Greta's deep focus on climate change became her cause. Her activism took a public turn when she sat outside Sweden's parliament for three weeks before the Swedish election in September 2018, holding a sign that read "Skolstrejk för Klimatet" (School Strike for Climate). This solitary act evolved into the global Fridays for Future movement, inspiring students worldwide to join her in striking for climate action.

Greta's advocacy work has taken her to big stages around the world, including the World Economic Forum and the United Nations. Her powerful speeches have made the world take notice of the urgent need to tackle climate change. Even when faced with criticism, she stays true to her mission. She is a true climate warrior. Beyond environmental activism, Greta has also used her platform to raise awareness about ASD, asserting that being different can be a superpower. Her life story serves as an inspiration for many, demonstrating that no one is too small to make a difference.

★Success Story Profile: Jackie Robinson★

Jackie Robinson, born in 1919 in Cairo, Georgia, was raised by his single mother, Mallie Robinson, in a family of sharecroppers.

Despite facing prejudice as the only black family on their block, their bond only strengthened. Jackie's humble beginnings led him to break Major League Baseball's color barrier that had segregated the sport for over 50 years.

From a young age, Jackie excelled in sports and became the first athlete at UCLA to win varsity letters in four sports: baseball, basketball, football, and track. His promising career was interrupted by financial difficulties and a stint in the U.S. Army. Robinson's activism began during his time in the military, where he was court-martialed for standing up against racial discrimination. However, in 1947, Jackie was approached by Brooklyn Dodgers president Branch Rickey to join the team, making him the first African-American player in the Major Leagues since 1889. This courageous act challenged the deeply rooted custom of racial segregation in America.

After his baseball career, he continued to advocate for civil rights, raising funds for the National Association for the Advancement of Colored People (NAACP) and the Southern Christian Leadership Conference (SCLC). He even hosted jazz concerts in his backyard to raise bail money for jailed activists.

Robinson's purpose as an athlete transcended winning games. He broke barriers, challenged societal norms, and used his influence to fight for equality. His life serves as a testament to the power of purpose, demonstrating that your passion can lead to significant societal change. His legacy continues to inspire individuals to stand up for what they believe in and strive for a better world.

★*Success Story Profile: Jimmy Carter*★

President James "Jimmy" Carter, the 39th President of the United States, serves as an inspiring example of finding purpose and making a difference. His tenure from 1977 to 1981 was marked by efforts to promote peace, democracy, human rights, and economic and social development, earning him the Nobel Peace Prize in 2002.

Carter's commitment to service extended beyond his presidency. In 1984, he began volunteering with Habitat for Humanity, a non-profit organization founded in Americus, Georgia, close to his hometown of Plains. The organization helps homeowners build homes alongside volunteers, embodying the spirit of community and cooperation.

For more than 35 years, Carter and his wife, former First Lady Rosalynn Carter, have been devoted volunteers with Habitat for Humanity. Through the Jimmy and Rosalynn Carter Work Project, they have been more than just advocates for affordable housing - they have also been active fundraisers and hands-on volunteers in construction. More than 4,300 homes could be considered a "Carter House" because the Carters have helped build that many homes with more than 100,000 volunteers in 14 countries over nearly 40 years, according to the organization.

Chapter Checklist: Find Your Purpose

The Bernie Sanders campaign, a beacon of purpose and passion, inspired millions to engage in their communities and foster positive change. This chapter, drawing inspiration from Sanders, provides exercises, tips, and success stories to help you identify your passion, recognize your talents, and define your mission. It guides you in creating a personalized purpose statement and emphasizes the importance of envisioning a future for all. The chapter illustrates how the synergy of passion, talent, mission, and reward can power a purpose-driven life. Your next step is to continue your journey into your community to research and locate local resources, networks, and people with common causes. Let us review the lessons learned in this chapter.

Checklist:

1. You explored exercises to understand what fuels your purpose. This is the first step in your journey toward achieving your life purpose with Ikigai.
2. You discovered your skills, talents, and superpowers, and how they can be used to help others, contributing to your sense of purpose.
3. You identified the types of work you love to do, learned how to perform your passion, and understood potential pitfalls.
4. You explored various causes and decided whether to focus on one or find commonality across multiple issues. You determined the results you wanted your work to produce, learned about possible mission missteps, and understood how to accomplish your mission.
5. You are aligned with what makes you happy to maintain balance and avoid burnout.
6. You developed a mission statement that combines your passions, skills and talents, mission, and rewards to summarize your purpose. This guides your next step in finding others in your community with a common purpose.
7. You also learned about the success stories of people like Danny Glover, Greta Thunberg, Jackie Robinson, and Jimmy Carter who have led lives of purpose, showcasing how passion, talent, mission, and reward can come together in powerful ways.

Two

Get Involved

Service to others is the rent you pay for your room here on Earth.
—Muhammad Ali

Muhammad Ali, a boxer, humanitarian, and social activist, was born Cassius Marcellus Clay Jr., on January 17, 1942, in Louisville, Kentucky. He was a champion in the sports world and a powerful voice against social injustices. Ali made history as the first fighter to win the world heavyweight championship three times and successfully defended this title 19 times. His legacy both inside and outside of the ring continues to inspire people worldwide.

Ali's life was marked by his unwavering stand against systemic oppression. In 1967, during the Vietnam War, Muhammad Ali was drafted to fight. However, citing his faith, he refused to serve in the U.S. Armed Forces. This decision led to severe repercussions: he was stripped of his heavyweight title, suspended from boxing, fined $10,000, and sentenced to five years in prison. While his stance sparked controversy, it also ignited a conversation about individual roles in societal issues. Ali remained steadfast in his beliefs.

This chapter draws inspiration from Ali's life, his commitment to serving his community, and his legacy. His quote, *"Service to others is the rent you pay for your room here on earth,"* encapsulates the essence of finding and serving your community. His legacy continues to inspire millions worldwide. The Muhammad Ali Center encourages everyone to make a difference in their communities and the world, sharing Ali's life as a tribute to the power of standing up for your beliefs.

After finding your purpose, it is time to find others who feel the same way. This chapter will guide you to connect with and serve your community. You will learn how to research local organizations, candidates, campaigns, and causes that align with your purpose and engage with them meaningfully. Here are some ways to connect with your community and find people who share your interests:

- **Find people with a common purpose:** Seek out people in your community who share your interests.
- **Attend community events:** Participate in local events to learn, network, stay informed, and voice your opinions.
- **Volunteer:** Donate your time and skills at a local food bank, school, or community center.
- **Join a local group or club:** Engage with groups that align with your interests and contribute to your community.
- **Contribute to local nonprofits:** Contribute to local nonprofits as a volunteer, donor, or board member.
- **Support a candidate:** If politics is your passion, consider supporting a campaign to learn more about the process and prepare for a potential run for office.

By the end of this chapter, you will have a deeper understanding of your community's needs, opportunities for involvement, and how to engage with local organizations and grassroots networks.

Find Your People

The first step towards community involvement is to connect with local groups that align with your interests. You can find these groups online or at local venues such as libraries, community centers, schools, or colleges. Remember to keep a record of this information for future use.

Identify key stakeholders in your community who are interested in the issues you care about. These could include civic groups, clubs, schools, college campuses, retirement centers, political groups, media, artists, writers, workers, small business owners, and community leaders. Reach out to everyone - from faith groups and women's groups to high school and college students, YMCA members, teachers, nurses, unions, and more. Understanding the needs of your community is crucial to serving them effectively.

College campuses are often hubs of activism and can be great places for outreach. Many communities have colleges with a history of student activism and local chapters of national organizations.

Networking with community service leaders whose work aligns with your purpose can be beneficial. If you are considering running for office, seek out a volunteer leadership position or training opportunity with a non-profit focused on your priorities.

Research local organizations in your community that align with your primary issues and purpose. Leadership development programs are also available within local government or groups. Volunteering with these entities can offer valuable insights into their operations and needs. To get involved, consider offering your services. This will enable you to understand more about the organization and its leaders. Ask yourself, what are the needs of the organization?

Understanding these needs can help you contribute effectively. Do they need help with fundraising? Can you donate? Is there a need for a leadership commitment on the board?

Attend Community Events

Participating in community events, forums, and conferences is an excellent way to connect with like-minded individuals in your community. It is not just about listening to speakers, but also about actively engaging and forming relationships. As you build new relationships and contacts, create a contact system and a directory with contact information, notes, links, and if possible, photos to help you remember everyone you meet.

 Tip

> Attend conferences to network with community leaders. You may be surprised to find many people in your community already actively supporting important causes.
>
> 1. **Research:** Look for conferences that align with your purpose statement. These events could be organized by local community groups, non-profit organizations, or professional associations. Find these events through online resources, community bulletin boards, or local newspapers.
>
> 2. **Plan:** Once you have identified a conference to attend, plan your visit. This could include arranging transpor-

tation, accommodation (if necessary), and understanding the conference schedule.

3. **Prepare:** Get to know the key speakers and topics that will be discussed at the conference. This will help you maximize the benefits of the sessions and discussions.

4. **Network:** Conferences provide excellent opportunities to meet individuals with similar interests and community leaders. Do not hesitate to introduce yourself and engage in conversations. Remember to bring business cards.

5. **Follow up:** After the conference, stay in touch with the people you have met. This could be through emails, phone calls, or even scheduling in-person meetings.

You should build and nurture relationships with people who share your interests, goals, or values. Networking can open opportunities, provide resources, offer support, and inspire your campaign, candidate, or cause.

 Tip

Networking is an important skill to make a difference in your community. Here are some tips to network effectively:

1. **Attend community events:** Participate in community events relevant to your mission. These could include

rallies, workshops, or social gatherings hosted by organizations or individuals you admire.

2. **Prepare introduction**: Craft a concise introduction that includes your name, affiliations, and purpose statement. Ensure it is clear, and brief, and encourages further conversation.

3. **Bring business cards**: Carry business cards to share your contact information. They should include your name, title, email, phone number, and any relevant web or social media links. A logo or photo can be a nice touch.

4. **Create a bookmark card**: If you're an author, consider a bookmark-style business card. It could feature your photo, name, and book title on one side, with your contact details and website on the other. This is a creative way to promote yourself and your work.

★*Success Story Profile: AARP*★

AARP is a nonprofit organization dedicated to empowering individuals to choose how they live as they age. It offers numerous resources for community engagement, volunteering, and local event participation.

Ethel Percy founded AARP when she was 73 years old. She believed that everyone had some good to do. "*The challenge is to live up to our better selves, to believe well of our fellow men and perhaps by doing so to help create the good, to experiment, to explore, to change, and to grow.*" These inspiring words were spoken by a long-time educator who made history as the first woman high school principal in California. Her contributions to society were recognized in 1993 when she was inducted into the National Women's Hall of Fame.

AARP can help you find people in your community and create good online community programs and events.

- Find local opportunities that match your skills and interests and search by cause, program, and opportunity.
- Search for ways to share your experience with the Volunteer Opportunity Board.
- Get ideas, inspiration, info and resources.
- Search for ways to share your experience with the community.

Volunteer In Your Community

Volunteering for a local campaign, candidate, or cause is an excellent way to connect with others and make a difference in your community. No matter the role, there is a place for you in non-profit organizations. They are always in need of volunteers to meet the diverse needs of the community.

 Tip

To find volunteer roles that suit your interests and skills, try matching your Ikigai self-assessment with the needs of local non-profit organizations. Here are some steps to guide you:

1. **Find your cause**: Choose a cause that resonates with

your values and interests. This could be anything from animal welfare to healthcare reform.
2. **Research**: Understand the mission, vision, and goals of potential organizations. Use their websites and social media for information.
3. **Assess your skills**: Evaluate your skills and consider how they could benefit the organizations you're interested in. Your talents and experiences can significantly contribute to the cause.
4. **Explore roles**: Reach out to the organizations for information on volunteer opportunities. Learn about the roles, responsibilities, and required skills. Inquire about the time commitment and benefits of volunteering.
5. **Apply and interview**: Once you've found a suitable role, apply as per the organization's guidelines. This may include filling out a form, submitting a resume, or providing references. An interview may follow where you can highlight your skills and passion.

★Success Story Profile: Volunteer Match★

The mission of VolunteerMatch.org is to change lives by connecting people in communities through service for passion, purpose, camaraderie, and hope, and experiencing joy and gratitude for the greater good is a great place to start your search.

This organization provides a platform to match your profile to your purpose statement reflecting your causes, skills, and location for volunteer opportunities in your community in person and online. The platform even provides personal recommendations to help you find your match.

As you educate yourself on local issues and needs, you can attend local events, either in person or online, to learn about active groups in your community that align with your focus. Research online, attend meetings, introduce yourself, and consider joining these groups. If no such group exists in your community, consider creating your own. This proactive approach not only helps you match your purpose statement with suitable causes but also provides a platform for you to make a tangible impact in your community.

★Success Story Profile: AmeriCorps★

AmeriCorps is a US federal agency that offers opportunities for adults to engage in local challenges with local solutions. The problem addresses opportunities in six areas: education, economic opportunity, disaster services, environmental stewardship, healthy futures, and veterans and military families to empower people to make a difference in the community.

The platform serves a network with over 1 million people and provides an environment to create relationships, develop personal and professional skills, and make a difference with benefits that vary across the different programs. career development. For older Americans, the platform provides the opportunity to share experience and a wealth of lifetime knowledge in new settings and areas of community need.

Join A Local Group or Club

An important step in your journey is to become a member of a local group or club that aligns with your interests and is active in your community. These organizations have resources and structures that can help form the foundation of your local organization and integrate you into a grassroots network. If you identify a need for a new community organization, don't hesitate to initiate one with friends and neighbors who share your interests. As Margaret Mead said, "*Never doubt that a small group of thoughtful, committed citizens can change the world; indeed, it's the only thing that ever has.*" Your efforts can significantly impact your community.

Many national organizations have local chapters that align with various volunteer interests. Investigate organizations online to find one that aligns with your interests. There are many causes to choose from, including animal welfare, anti-racism and discrimination, democratic reform, environmental justice, gun violence prevention, elections and voting rights, food security and anti-poverty, campaign finance reform, civil rights, climate change, community safety and wellness, criminal justice reform, economic inequality, education reform, and freedom of speech, press, and protest. In the next section, you will explore specific areas of interest and find organizations that work in these fields.

Animal Welfare

Animal rights organizations encompass a wide range of entities, from animal rescues, shelters, and sanctuaries to legal outreach groups advocating for policy change. There are many organizations dedicated to animal welfare, including anti-poaching groups, humane societies, spay and neuter clinics, and research centers.

- **American Society for the Prevention of Cruelty to Animals:** As the first humane society in North America, it has grown to be one of the largest, with over 2 million supporters nationwide. The ASPCA's mission is to provide effective means for preventing cruelty to animals throughout the United States.

- **Best Friends:** Started as a humble sanctuary for homeless and special-needs animals, built from the ground up with passion and a belief in a humane path forward with the power of kindness and compassion towards animals.
- **The Humane Society:** Fight to end suffering for all animals to achieve a humane society.
- **Mexipets:** US-based nonprofit organization dedicated to improving the welfare of cats and dogs in Mexico, primarily in the area of Maravatío, Michoacán.

Anti-Poverty and Food Security

These organizations address poverty, hunger, and food insecurity, empower communities, and provide resources to those in need through food banks, gleaning organizations, farmer's markets, community gardens, and affordable housing initiatives. They help bridge the gap by providing resources to those in need. Food pantries, for example, offer food, personal hygiene items, towels, and detergent.

- **Association of Gleaning Organizations.** A member-led network that builds the capacity of organizations to recover surplus fruits and vegetables, reducing waste and aiding vulnerable populations' food access. Their mission engages communities in harvesting surplus produce for those in need. The adaptable, sustainable network aims to be a hub supporting gleaning organizations, educating the public and funding resources, facilitating networking, communication among members, and sharing funding and programmatic resources.
- **Bethlehem House of Bread** provides neighbors in the community who are hungry with healthy and nutritious food to

thrive with the message, "*A well-fed community is better for us all.*" The mission is to feed those who are hungry in body and spirit at a table where all are welcome. We understand that life happens, but hunger shouldn't. Every day, hundreds of our neighbors don't know where their next meal will come from, and we're here to help them.

- **Oregon Food Bank.** The mission is to eliminate hunger and its root causes in Oregon and Southwest Washington. The Oregon Food Bank cultivates a community-led network of people fighting hunger at every level. The Oregon Food Bank provides food and food subsidies, establishes community programs that address food insecurity, and supports other organizations throughout Oregon with their network of services.
- **Portland Fruit Tree Project** is a grassroots organization that provides a community-based solution to a critical and growing need in Portland and beyond with access to healthy food.

★*Success Story Profile: Portland Fruit Tree Project*★

The Portland Fruit Tree Project is a grassroots non-profit organization that empowers neighbors to share in the harvest and care of urban fruit trees. They provide a community-based solution to a critical and growing need in Portland and beyond access to healthy food and the benefits provided by trees including cleaner air, shade, and food. By empowering neighbors to share in the harvest and care of urban fruit trees, they are preventing waste, building community knowledge and resources, and creating sustainable ways to obtain healthy, locally grown food. They address food insecurity and environmental issues in Portland and beyond by providing access to healthy food and creating sustainable ways to obtain locally-grown food.

Their vision statement is, *"We envision joyful communities that see every fruit tree as an abundant resource that contributes to a just food system and enhances the well-being of people, community networks, habitat, and our changing climate."*

In a creative twist, the organization set a new world record for the world's largest charcuterie board, aptly named the "CharFruit-Tree" board. This event was a major fundraiser celebrating the 2023 harvest season. The 500-foot board was designed to break all known records for the longest ever assembled featuring community partners, sponsors, and volunteers.

This innovative approach not only raised awareness but also funds for the organization's mission. The Portland Fruit Tree Project exemplifies how creative solutions can address critical community needs.

Anti-Racism and Civil Rights

Anti-racism and civil rights organizations are dedicated to advancing equality, protecting civil liberties, and combating racial discrimination.

- **American Civil Liberties Union (ACLU):** The ACLU has evolved from a small group into the leading defender of rights protected by the U.S. Constitution. With over 1.7 million members, 500 staff attorneys, thousands of volunteer attorneys, and offices across the country, the ACLU tirelessly fights against government abuse and staunchly defends individual freedoms. These include speech and religion, a woman's right to choose the right to due process, and citizens' rights to privacy.

- **Black Youth Project:** The Black Youth Project focuses on studying the attitudes, resources, and culture of young, urban black millennials. It explores how these elements influence their decision-making, norms, and behavior in critical areas such as sex, health, and politics. The project aims to understand the unique challenges and choices confronting African-American youth in the post–civil rights era.
- **Las Americas Immigrant Advocacy Center:** Committed to offering high-quality legal services to low-income immigrants and advocating for human rights. The organization envisions a nation where all immigrants have access to top-notch legal representation, thereby upholding justice and human rights.
- **National Association for the Advancement of Colored People:** The NAACP is a grassroots organization committed to advocating for the civil rights of Black America. Building on the legacy of civil rights pioneers like W.E.B. Du Bois, Ida B. Wells, and Thurgood Marshall, the NAACP works in cities, schools, companies, and courtrooms nationwide. The organization aims to create an inclusive community where everyone can exercise their civil and human rights without discrimination. Committed to a world without racism, the NAACP strives to ensure that Black people enjoy equitable opportunities in thriving communities.
- **Southern Poverty Law Center:** Dedicated to fighting hate and hard right extremism, the SPLC monitors over 1,300 extremist groups operating across the country, including the Ku Klux Klan, the neo-Nazi movement, neo-Confederates, racist skinheads, antigovernment militias, and others. The

organization exposes these groups' activities to the public, media, and policymakers through investigative reports and expert analysis. The SPLC also supports grassroots partners to intervene earlier in pushing white supremacy out of the mainstream and remedying harms in communities.

Democratic Reform

Many organizations are committed to democratic reform and progressive policies with chapters in local communities across the US. These organizations promote progressive policies, reform democracy, build grassroots movements, and encourage inclusivity.

- Democratic Socialists of America (DSA) is working towards a more free, democratic, and humane society.
- Indivisible is a movement of thousands of group leaders and more than a million members taking regular, iterative, and increasingly complex actions to resist the GOP's agenda, elect local champions, and fight for progressive policies.
- Our Revolution is organizing a political revolution to challenge the power of big money and prioritize the needs of people and our planet. The mission is to educate voters about issues, get people involved in the political process, and work to organize and elect progressive candidates.

★*Success Story Profile: Our Revolution East Bay*★

Our Revolution is a progressive political action organization formed after Bernie Sanders's 2016 presidential campaign. The goal is to organize a national network of state and local grassroots groups to fight for change from the bottom up; holding politicians in power accountable to putting the needs of working Americans; fighting for progressive policies and taking on corporate power to win health care for all, worker rights, climate justice, voting rights, and more; electing progressive champions up and down the ballot - from county commissioners to Members of Congress like Representatives Alexandria Ocasio-Cortez and Cori Bush; and transforming the Democratic Party into a more progressive party by challenging the influence of the establishment and its big money donors.

Our Revolution East Bay, a local Our Revolution group, started as a small group of volunteers known as Berkeley for Bernie and has grown in just a few years into a powerful grassroots force in the Alameda and Contra Costa counties in California. They are active in local East Bay elections, canvassing and phone-banking for mayoral and city council candidates as well as for progressive ballot measures, and working to reform the Democratic Party.

Their success story serves as an inspiring example for those looking to join or form a group in their community. The Our Revolution East Bay volunteers use many creative strategies and tactics to engage with the community, expand membership, and achieve goals:

- Hosting meetings and events for speakers to share important campaigns for local, state, and federal candidates for office, as well as endorsing the candidates that met their criteria.
- Using digital communications such as weekly newsletters and social media to inform and mobilize their members and supporters.
- Tabling at farmers markets, rallies, and on public transportation to encourage voters for key elections and candidates with fun and creative signs and group songs.
- Creating catchy and colorful messaging and graphics on signs, banners, flyers, and digital media to attract attention

and spread awareness about their causes and candidates. They distributed their flyers on bulletin boards in coffee shops and doors when canvassing the community.

Climate Action and Environmental Justice

There are many organizations committed to fighting climate change and promoting environmental sustainability. They believe in the power of grassroots movements to influence policy and action for environmental justice and sustainability.

- **350.org:** This organization works to end the age of fossil fuels and build a world with community-centered renewable energy for all. It runs grassroots campaigns worldwide to raise awareness and demand action on climate change.
- **Food & Water Watch:** Mobilizes regular people to build political power to move bold and uncompromised solutions to the most pressing food, water, and climate problems of our time. It works to protect people's health, communities, and democracy from the growing destructive power of the most powerful economic interests.
- **Greenpeace:** Dedicated to preserving endangered species of animals, preventing environmental abuses, and heightening environmental awareness. It uses non-violent and creative campaigns to highlight global environmental problems and advocate for solutions.
- **Sierra Club:** Mission to explore, enjoy, and protect the wild places of the earth; practice and promote the responsible use of the earth's ecosystems and resources; educate and enlist humanity to protect and restore the quality of the natural

and human environment. It organizes outdoor activities, environmental campaigns, and political advocacy.
- **Subject to Climate:** Provides K-12 educators with free, credible, and engaging materials on climate change, with an emphasis on interdisciplinary climate change education. It encourages teachers of all subjects and grade levels to incorporate climate change into their lessons, not to teach climate science in every class, but to encourage gradual, developmentally appropriate incorporations of climate change in each classroom.
- **Sunrise Movement:** Fighting to stop the climate crisis and win a Green New Deal. This organization is creating a movement to transition to 100% clean energy for everyone. They organize strikes, rallies, and trainings to mobilize young people and urge politicians to act on climate change.

★*Success Story Profile: Sunrise Movement*★

Sunrise Movement, formed in 2017, is a collective youth-led effort to halt climate change and create millions of good jobs through a Green New Deal. The founders, veterans of the youth climate movement, envisioned a movement as massive as the crisis we face. Their vision extends beyond a new bill in Congress; it's about creating a livable future for all, ensuring every person's right to clean air and water, protection from disaster, access to healthy food, and a comfortable life.

The Green New Deal aims to transform American society and economy to achieve 100% clean and renewable energy within the next decade. The Green New Deal for Schools initiative empowers students across the country to advocate for safe, clean, and climate-prepared schools. It calls on school boards and superintendents to pass district-wide policies while building momentum for federal legislation.

In 2023, the Sunrise Movement's relentless advocacy led to President Biden announcing the American Climate Corps program. This initiative serves as a major green jobs training program and is expected to employ over 20,000 individuals for conservation work. Despite this achievement, the Sunrise Movement acknowledges the ongoing work needed in transitioning from fossil fuels to renewable energy. The organization continues to hold politicians accountable and fight for progressive policies, underscoring the power of grassroots organizing in effecting national change.

Gun Violence Prevention Advocacy

These organizations are fighting to save lives by advocating for gun violence prevention.

- **Brady United:** A movement named after Jim and Sarah Brady, who passed the bipartisan Brady Law in 1993, that is dedicated to addressing America's gun violence epidemic.
- **Everytown for Gun Safety:** This organization advocates for policies like universal background checks and stricter firearm sale and ownership regulations to reduce gun violence in America.
- **Giffords**: This group challenges the gun lobby, holds elected officials accountable, and advocates for safer laws to prevent gun violence at all government levels.
- **Moms Demand Action:** A grassroots network advocating for public safety measures to protect people from gun violence.
- **Sandy Hook Promise:** A non-profit aiming to prevent

- gun-related deaths due to crime, suicide, and accidental discharge to prevent parents from experiencing the horrific loss of their child.
- **Students Demand Action:** A national organization formed by U.S. high school and college students in response to the 2018 mass shooting at Marjory Stoneman Douglas High School. With over 600 groups nationwide, it's committed to ending gun violence and effecting meaningful legislative change.

★Success Story Profile: March for Our Lives★

March for Our Lives is a movement led by young people, born out of the tragic school shooting at Marjory Stoneman Douglas High School in Parkland, Florida. Its mission is to encourage civic engagement, education, and direct action to end gun violence. Their goal is to create safe and healthy communities where gun violence is obsolete.

In response to the shooting, the movement organized the largest single-day protest against gun violence in history. Millions united to protest political leaders' inaction, marking a significant step in their mission to ensure no community experiences such a tragedy again. Their efforts underscore the power of youth activism and collective action in effecting change at a national level.

Election and Voting Rights

These organizations are doing important work to protect voting rights and ensure free, fair, and secure elections in the United States.

- **Common Cause:** This nonpartisan organization supports efforts at all levels to strengthen our democracy and uphold

American democratic values. It aims to empower everyone to have their voices heard in the political process.
- **Headcount:** A non-partisan organization that uses the power of music to register voters and encourage democratic participation.
- **Independent Voter Project:** Seeks to re-engage nonpartisan voters and promote nonpartisan election reform through initiatives, litigation, and voter education.
- **League of Women Voters:** Founded by suffrage movement leaders in 1920, this organization works on voter registration for all people. Their online voter education tool, vote 411, provides important information about voting options, requirements, registration deadlines, and polling locations.
- **Rock the Vote:** Started by music executives in response to the censorship of hip-hop music, this nonpartisan group taps into the power of young people to build their political power through voter registration efforts and reducing barriers to vote.

Freedom of Speech, Press, and Protest

Freedom of speech, press, and the right to protest and assemble are fundamental rights that underpin our democratic society. They enable the open exchange of ideas, hold those in power accountable, and allow citizens to express their views and advocate for change. Many organizations play a key role in upholding these democratic values by ensuring these fundamental freedoms are protected and respected.

- **Berkelyside, Oaklandside, and Richmondside:** Cityside Journalism, which includes Berkelyside, Oaklandside, and

Richmondside, is a nonpartisan, nonprofit media organization dedicated to building community through local journalism. They serve local communities with high-quality reporting and civic engagement.
- **California Writers Club:** Non-profit organization for writers.
- **Foundation for Individual Rights and Expression:** A non-profit civil liberties group that protects free speech rights on college campuses in the United States.
- **National Writers Union:** A labor union that represents freelance writers working in all genres, formats, and mediums. The union works to advance the economic status and working conditions of writers.
- **Willamette Writers:** Non-profit educational organization dedicated to helping writers connect with their communities and develop their craft.

Sports for Good

There are many non-profit cause organizations for good with a focus on how sports, physical exercise, getting outdoors, and life lessons from teams, players, coaches, and physical fitness are good for people. Here are a few organizations with this mission and purpose:

- **Ali Center:** The Muhammad Ali Center is much more than a museum. As an athlete, a humanitarian, a global voice, and a man guided by faith, Muhammad Ali embodied a pursuit and belief in the greatness found in all people. Founded in 2005 by Lonnie and Muhammad Ali in his hometown of Louisville, the Center is dedicated to honoring Ali and continuing work based on his core principles. The mission is to mobilize Muhammad Ali's legacy to foster respect, inspire generations of changemakers, advance social justice, and envision a just and compassionate world where all people can reach their greatness.

- **Athletes for Hope:** This organization educates athletes on their potential to make a positive impact on the world, connects them with the causes they care about, and inspires others to do the same. They work with over 8,000 athlete members from various sports and levels to engage in charitable activities and causes.
- **Diveheart Foundation:** This organization uses scuba diving as a tool to help people with disabilities improve their self-esteem, confidence, and independence. They provide scuba diving training, trips, and experiences for people of all ages and abilities, including veterans, children, and adults with physical or mental challenges.
- **Sierra Club Local Outings:** Local Outings volunteers lead a range of outings that are as diverse as their interests from paddling to picnics, day hikes to camping trips, bicycling, skiing, paddling, birdwatching, conservation-oriented activities, and trips into the remaining natural areas in our communities.

 Tip

Volunteering in youth sports can be a fulfilling way to share your passion, skills, and experience. It can also boost your physical health, mental well-being, social skills, and life skills. Here is a tip to get you started:

1. **Choose your sport or activity:** Select a sport or activity that you enjoy and suits your skills. Experiment with various sports or join a club to explore your interests. You could volunteer in sports like soccer, basketball, tennis, golf, cycling, hiking, or yoga.

2. **Volunteer:** Volunteer as a coach, mentor, or leader, using your knowledge and expertise to teach, guide, and inspire others.

3. **Seek support:** Do not hesitate to seek support and feedback from others. Coaches, mentors, friends, or family members experienced in your chosen sport can offer valuable advice.

4. **Have fun:** Volunteering in sports should be enjoyable. It is a chance to boost your physical health, enhance your mental well-being, develop social skills, and learn valuable life lessons.

Support Local Nonprofits

Serving as a volunteer, donor, or board member for local nonprofit organizations is a fantastic way to connect with others and make a difference. These organizations often lead the way in addressing community needs, advocating for change, and providing essential services. Your involvement can contribute to their mission and provide you with valuable experience, connections, and understanding of the issues at hand. This hands-on experience can shape your perspective and approach when you decide to run for office. Here are five steps you can take to support local nonprofits:

- **Volunteer your time:** Offer your skills and time to the nonprofit. This could involve anything from helping at events to providing services and your skills and expertise.
- **Donate:** If you have the means, final donations are always appreciated. Even small contributions can go a long way in supporting a nonprofit's mission.
- **Join the board:** If you're able to make a longer-term commitment, consider joining the nonprofit's board of directors. This can provide valuable leadership experience.
- **Fundraise:** Help raise money for the nonprofit by organizing a fundraising event or campaign. This not only raises funds but also awareness for the cause.
- **Spread the word:** Share your experiences with friends, family, and social networks to encourage others to get involved as well.

Volunteer for a Candidate or an Elected Official

If politics is your passion, volunteering for a candidate's campaign is an excellent way to gain experience and learn about the political process. Start by researching local candidates running for positions such as school boards, city councils, state legislatures, and Congress.

Local candidates often provide excellent opportunities for volunteering, donating, and supporting their campaigns. As a volunteer, you can assist with tasks such as organizing canvassing, phone and text banking, digital and social media outreach, event organization, community outreach, and fundraising.

If you are considering running for office or seeking an elected political position, it is helpful to first engage with local organizations in your community. Attend meetings of the city council or school board to learn from existing members. Make introductions to others attending the meeting, including elected officials and attendees. Consider reaching out to previously elected officials and community leaders for an introductory coffee meeting.

Start local in your neighborhood or city and then expand regionally, and statewide. Use your written purpose and passion statement as the basis for an introduction flyer and your concise elevator pitch to share your ideas with others in person and online. If you're ready to become a candidate, start by introducing yourself to members of community groups who share common values and are focused on similar issues and causes that will become an important part of your campaign.

 Tip

> Supporting local candidates in your political engagement journey can provide valuable experience and insights into your community's workings. This hands-on experience is crucial for understanding your constituents' needs and challenges. Here are five actions you can take to get involved with a candidate or local political leader, build your experience, and learn about running for office:
>
> 1. **Volunteer**: Contribute your time and skills to a campaign. This could involve a range of activities from

door-knocking and phone banking to data entry and event planning.

2. **Attend local meetings**: Attend city council or county commission meetings, town halls, school board meetings, and other public forums. This will give you a sense of the current issues, debates, and important leaders in your community.

3. **Network**: Connect with local leaders, activists, and community members. Building relationships can open doors to opportunities and collaborations.

4. **Educate yourself**: Knowledge is power when it comes to making informed decisions and advocating for change. Read local news sources, research problems, and policies, and listen to constituents' concerns.

5. **Speak up**: Use your voice to advocate for issues you care about. Whether it's through social media, at a public meeting, or in a letter to the editor of your local newspaper, speaking up can influence public opinion and policy.

Chapter Checklist: Get Involved

The story of Muhammad Ali serves as an inspiring example of someone who embodied a pursuit and belief in the greatness found in all people. His legacy and purpose are reflected in the resources, tips, and success story profiles of this chapter.

Checklist:

In this chapter, you gained a deeper understanding of your community's needs and learned how to get involved and make a difference through local organizations and grassroots networks.

1. You connected with people in your community who shared your interests for support, inspiration, and potential collaboration.
2. You actively participated in community events to broaden your knowledge, expand your network, and engage in meaningful discussions.
3. You volunteered at local organizations, leveraging your unique skills to make a significant impact and gain valuable experience.
4. You joined local groups or clubs that align with your interests, further enriching your community involvement.
5. You supported local nonprofits through volunteering, donations, or board membership, aiding in their crucial work.
6. You delved into politics by volunteering for a candidate's campaign, gaining insights into the political process, and preparing for potential future candidacy.

Three

Create Your Plan

By failing to plan, you are planning to fail.
—Benjamin Franklin

Benjamin Franklin, born in Boston in 1706, had many skills and achievements. He started as an apprentice to his brother James, a printer, which led to his success as a printer in Philadelphia. His curiosity made him a famous scientist, known for his electricity experiments and inventions like the lightning rod, bifocals, and the Franklin stove.

His contributions extended far beyond science and invention. He was a civic activist at heart, founding many organizations that shaped colonial and revolutionary Philadelphia. He was involved in creating the Library Company of Philadelphia, Pennsylvania Hospital, and what is now the University of Pennsylvania. His belief in community and working together showed in his leadership roles in government, from serving as a clerk in the Pennsylvania Assembly to a commissioner to France during the Revolution. Franklin played a key role in the American Revolution. His diplomatic skills were crucial in securing French support, which was instrumental in the victory of the American colonies over Great Britain. His efforts epitomize the importance of careful planning and strategic alliances in effecting change.

Inspired by Benjamin Franklin's wisdom, this chapter guides you to build upon the reflections and actions from previous chapters. It will help you formulate a robust plan for your campaign, candidate, or cause, underlining the importance of strategic planning for success. In this chapter, you will build on the reflections and actions from the previous chapters to create a plan for your campaign, candidate, or cause. After engaging with your community, the next step is to collaborate and formulate your plan. This plan will translate your vision into a strategy with clear goals and objectives, outlining the specific actions needed to achieve your desired outcomes. Every initiative should have a plan - a dynamic document with milestones and annual reviews. Ideally, you'll work closely with your team to complete this chapter's steps and connect with others who share your passion, learning from their feedback.

This chapter provides an overview of the planning process, including templates, examples, and best practices. Your plan will encompass your vision and strategy, mission statement, strategic goals and objectives, and a variety of tactics across both in-person and online engagement channels.

Your plan empowers you to be creative and design a strategic approach as you navigate challenges, constraints, and conflicts. With a clear plan in hand, you can evaluate roadblocks, anticipate challenges, and consider alternate courses of action. By setting milestones and deadlines, you hold yourself accountable and can allocate resources accordingly. Your plan provides a higher-level view of your strategies and the necessary tactics and operations, empowering you to make decisions aligned with your long-term goals.

Your plan is also your most valuable tool for communication and collaboration. It helps provide a common understanding of your objectives and milestones, encouraging unity and engagement in your community. Clear deadlines and objectives help with the effective delegation of tasks, promoting accountability and teamwork. Share your plan as it evolves with your team for feedback, understanding, and collective ownership. This transparency will encourage open conversation, and new ideas, and lead to a better plan to achieve your goals. Here are the steps to create your plan:

- **Define your vision and strategy:** Develop a strategy that aligns with your purpose and mission, considering your goals and available resources.
- **Engage your team**: Establish a structured organization with clear roles, community agreements, and a well-defined agenda to foster a respectful and collaborative environment.
- **Set goals**: Create goals that are specific, measurable, achievable, relevant, time-bound, inclusive, and equitable.
- **Identify target audience**: Determine your target audience for your campaign, candidate, or cause to help segment your audience, and tailor your goals and objectives.
- **Outline tactics**: Develop a balanced mix of tactics and actions suitable for your campaign, candidate, or cause plan.
- **Measure success**: As you transition from planning to implementation, set metrics for your goals and expected outcomes, reviewing them periodically to reassess your objectives.

Your Vision Statement

Begin writing a clear plan with your vision that encompasses your purpose statement developed in the first chapter. Your vision should map three to five years with a compelling vision for change supporting your campaign, candidate, or cause. When setting your vision and strategies, be creative, think big, and outside the box. Your vision should be ambitious enough to make a difference but with targeted strategies that can be focused targets to have the chance to win.

 **Tip**

> Create a vision statement that describes your desired future state in 3 to 5 years, based on the purpose statement that you created in Chapter 1. The vision statement should be clear, concise, and inspiring. To create a vision statement, you can:
>
> 1. Review your purpose statement and identify the core values, goals, and impact that you want to achieve.
>
> 2. Imagine how the world or your community would be if you achieved your purpose and goals.
>
> 3. Write a couple of sentences that describe your vision in a hopeful, inspiring, and persuasive way.
>
> 4. Use specific and vivid language that appeals to the emotions and senses of your audience.
>
> 5. Revise and refine your vision statement until it is clear, concise, and inspiring.

Here are some examples of vision statements for a campaign, a candidate, and a cause:

- **"Save the Forests" campaign vision statement:** In 5 years, a world where forests are protected and restored as vital ecosystems that support biodiversity, climate stability, and human well-being.

- **"School board" candidate vision statement:** In 5 years, a school district that provides high-quality education for all students, regardless of their background, abilities, or needs.

- **"Anti-poverty" cause vision statement:** In 5 years, a community where poverty is significantly reduced or eradicated, achieved through collective action, empowerment, and a shared commitment to ensure access to essential resources for all members of our community.".

★Success Story Profile: Habitat for Humanity★

Habitat for Humanity is a global nonprofit housing organization that works with local communities to provide decent and affordable shelter for families in need. Habitat's vision statement is: *"A world where everyone has a decent place to live."* This vision statement is effective because it is:

- **Inspirational:** It motivates people to work together towards the shared goal of bettering the lives of millions worldwide.
- **Aspirational:** It reflects the highest ideals and dreams of the organization, not just its current reality or capabilities.
- **Imaginative:** It creates a vivid mental image of the future state that the organization wants to create or contribute to, where everyone has a safe and comfortable home.
- **Specific:** It uses clear and concrete language that relates to

the cause of housing and distinguishes the organization from others that may have similar goals.

Habitat's vision statement supports its mission statement, which describes how the organization will achieve its vision: "*To bring people together to build homes, communities, and hope.*" Habitat's mission statement explains the main activities and strategies of the organization, such as building homes, fostering community partnerships, and inspiring hope among families and volunteers.

Habitat's vision and mission statements are both concise and compelling, capturing the essence of the organization's purpose and impact in one sentence or phrase. They are also easy to remember and communicate to others, as they use simple and direct words. They are not too vague or abstract, as they specify the target group (everyone), the main issue (housing), and the desired outcome (decent place to live).

Engage Your Team

Start by assembling your core team to draft your plan. Ensure your meetings and collaborations are accessible, inclusive, equitable, and just. This includes having clear roles, decision processes, and accountability.

Involve your team in setting goals and strategies for your plan. Deadlines can help maintain focus and drive. Remember, team members come from diverse backgrounds and have different strengths. Some excel at big-picture thinking, while others are task-oriented.

The process begins by bringing together your core team to work together to draft your plan. It is very important to follow accessible, inclusive, equitable, and just best practices for your meetings and collaboration. These include having clear roles, decision processes, and accountability. Consider these best practices for effective and inclusive meetings:

- **Assign roles**: Assign or volunteer roles for your meeting, such as facilitator, note-taker, timekeeper, or presenter.
- **Share goals**: People commit when they believe their efforts will make a difference. Share your goals with the team.
- **Create an agenda**: Decide on discussion topics, time allocation, and objectives. Share the agenda beforehand and invite suggestions.
- **Use a progressive stack**: This method decides who speaks next in a meeting, prioritizing those who haven't spoken yet, those from marginalized groups, or those with a different viewpoint.
- **Choose a decision-making process**: Select a process that suits your group and the decisions you need to make. Options include consensus, majority vote, or delegation.
- **Foster an open environment**: Encourage members to listen, brainstorm, and share their opinions and experiences. Respect diversity and avoid personal attacks and judgments.

Your team will be instrumental in co-drafting your plan, which can start as simple as brainstorming ideas on a napkin, poster paper in a conference room, or digital documentation online. Goals provide a framework and roles for the work that needs to be done. They help move your plan from a piece of paper or a document to a living organizational movement.

 Tip

Creating a goal-planning team is a crucial step in any campaign, candidate, or cause. Here are some tips and best practices for planning the meeting, norms, and how to create a structure for inclusive and productive conversations:

1. **Plan the meeting:** Set a clear agenda that includes the meeting's purpose, discussion topics, and desired outcomes. Ensure all team members have the necessary materials or information beforehand. Consider using a facilitator to guide the discussion.

2. **Set norms**: Establish norms to create a safe and respectful environment. This could include active listening, respecting diverse viewpoints, and maintaining confidentiality. Use strategies like round-robin sharing or anonymous suggestion boxes to ensure all voices are heard.

3. **Create structure**: Use a structured conversation to cover all topics and keep the discussion focused. Consider the SMARTIE model (Specific, Measurable, Achievable, Rewarding, Timely, Inclusive, Equitable) for setting goals. This provides a clear roadmap and ensures goals are actionable and aligned with the team's vision.

4. **Align goals with vision and strategy**: Ensure your team's goals align with the overall vision and strategy of your campaign, candidate, or cause. Regularly revisit your goals to ensure they remain relevant as circumstances change.

Effective team involvement in setting goals and strategies is crucial for success. By fostering a collaborative and respectful environment, you can leverage the collective strength of your team to make a significant impact in your community or on the planet. Plan your meetings with a clear purpose, desired outcome, and a structured plan to ensure productive discussions and tangible results.

 Tip

Use the Purpose, Outcome, and Process (POP) template for effective meetings. POP answers the w*hy, what, and how* of your meeting agenda and process.

1. **Explain the purpose of your meeting:** Define the reason and main objective of your meeting.

2. **Outcome**: Determine the specific achievements needed by the end of the meeting.

3. **Process**: Plan how the meeting will be run and what methods will be used to achieve the outcome.

4. **Resource alignment**: Strategize on using time, materials, and people effectively to reach your purpose and outcome.

5. **Focus**: Concentrate on the most important aspects of your meeting and avoid unnecessary distractions.

6. **Communication**: Share your POP with participants and stakeholders to gain their buy-in and feedback.

> 7. **Evaluation**: Measure and monitor your progress and success during and after the meeting, celebrating achievements and learning from challenges.

POP Template Examples

Here are some POP examples for a campaign, a candidate, and a cause:

Progressive environmental campaign

- **Purpose:** To create a campaign plan that addresses urgent environmental issues and mobilizes public support and action.
- **Outcome:** A vision and strategy with 3 goals, and outlines for relevant tactics and measurable outcomes for the campaign.
- **Plan:** An agenda with a series of short 50-minute meetings that include:
    - Introductions, norms, and roles
    - Discuss the vision statement.
    - Brainstorm 3 goals.
    - Outline tactics and measurements of success.
    - Decide the next steps.

Candidate for local office:

- **Purpose:** To run for local city council and represent the interests and needs of the community.
- **Outcome:** A strategy with objectives to win the election and implement positive changes in the city.
- **Plan:** A kickoff meeting with 5 volunteer leaders on the

election committee who will play roles advising the candidate and helping in areas of campaign manager, treasurer, communications and social media, and outreach. The meeting will cover:
- Candidate's background, values, and platform.
- Campaign budget and fundraising plan.
- Communication and social media strategy.
- Outreach and voter engagement plan.

Cause for community safety

- **Purpose:** To address community safety with concerns about traffic congestion, safe paths to schools, and agenda to engage city council leaders with specific issues.
- **Outcome:** A committee formed with representatives from different stakeholders, such as parents, teachers, students, residents, businesses, and city officials. A list of safety issues and solutions to present to the city council.
- **Plan:** A town hall meeting with the community to:
  - Raise awareness and generate interest in the cause.
  - Solicit feedback and input from the community members.
  - Identify potential committee members and leaders.
  - Prioritize safety issues and solutions.

Set Strategic Goals

Your goals should be clear, achievable, and motivating for your group. They should guide your daily actions and help you track your progress and success. Without a clear plan and roadmap, your organization might lose focus, momentum, and support. Your plan will help you turn your vision into reality by building and sustaining collective energy and power.

One way to create effective goals is to use the SMARTIE framework. Each goal should be:

- **Specific:** Define your goal clearly and concisely. Avoid vague or general statements.
- **Measurable:** Include precise amounts, dates, or indicators in your goal so you can track your performance and evaluate your outcomes.
- **Achievable:** Make sure your goal is realistic and attainable given the resources and time you have. Challenge yourself but don't set yourself up for failure.
- **Rewarding:** Choose a goal that is meaningful and motivating for you or your team. Celebrate your achievements and recognize your efforts.
- **Timely:** Set a clear timeline for your goal with a start and end date. Break down your goal into smaller milestones and deadlines to keep yourself on track.
- **Inclusive:** Consider all the stakeholders involved in or affected by your goal and make them feel valued and engaged. Seek input and feedback from diverse perspectives and experiences.
- **Equitable:** Ensure your goal promotes fairness and justice within your team or community. Address any barriers or biases that may hinder your progress or impact.

Here are a couple of examples of SMARTIE goals for a campaign, candidate, and cause.

- **Campaign:** Pass renewable energy legislation in our

community. Achieve 70% support from community members in the next public hearing. Gather 5000 signatures for our petition within the next six months. Host a community celebration once the legislation is passed. Achieve this within three years. Involve at least 10 local schools in our awareness campaign. Ensure all neighborhoods in our community benefit from this legislation.
- **Candidate:** Win the local school board election. Secure endorsements from at least three current board members. Knock on every door in our district before election day. Host a volunteer appreciation event after the election, regardless of the outcome. Achieve this within the current election cycle. Hold bi-weekly town halls to gather input from community members. Ensure our campaign staff and volunteers reflect the diversity of our district.
- **Cause:** Reduce litter in our local parks by 50%. Conduct monthly litter surveys to track progress. Organize weekly clean-up events with at least 20 volunteers each time. Plan a picnic celebration in the park once the goal is achieved. Achieve this within one year. Partner with local schools, businesses, and organizations for clean-up events. Distribute clean-up supplies for free to all volunteers.

Power Mapping

Power mapping is a valuable tool for analyzing and setting goals. To create effective goals, employ power mapping and theory of change methods. These methods aid in comprehending the power structures and dynamics impacting your cause or campaign, enabling you to influence them and achieve your desired change.

Power mapping involves identifying key actors or groups with the power to make decisions or influence outcomes related to your issue. It also assists in assessing their level of interest or support for your cause and determining effective ways to engage them. Power mapping helps answer questions such as:

- Who are the decision-makers that can approve or reject your proposal or demand?
- Who are the allies that can support or amplify your cause or campaign?
- Who are the opponents that can oppose or undermine your cause or campaign?
- Who are the influencers that can sway the opinions or actions of the decision-makers, allies, or opponents?
- Who are the targets that can benefit from or be affected by your cause or campaign?

You can use a power mapping tool to help define your target audience and create a visual representation of the power map for your campaign, candidate, or cause. List the actors or groups, their level of power, their level of interest or support, and your engagement strategy for each one.

Theory of Change

Your *theory of change* is a process to articulate the logic behind how your actions will lead to the change you want to see in the world. It helps you clarify your assumptions, identify your outcomes, and measure your impact. You can tell your theory of change story or narrative as part of your plan. A theory of change can help answer questions like:

- What is the problem or issue you want to tackle?

- What is the goal you are striving for?
- What are the intermediate outcomes or changes that need to happen along the way?
- What are the activities or tactics that you will use to achieve those outcomes?
- What are the assumptions or risks that underlie your theory of change?
- What are the indicators or evidence that will show that you have achieved your outcomes?

By using these methods, you can create strategic goals that are aligned with your vision and mission, informed by your power analysis, and guided by your theory of change. You can also monitor and evaluate your progress and impact using data and evidence.

Campaign strategic goals: Save the community forest

- In five years, reduce water runoff and prevent soil erosion effectively by 50% through the strategic planting and maintenance of trees. Trees, especially those on steeper hillsides, hold the soil in place, preventing erosion and improving water quality.
- In five years, increase the forest cover by 10% through reforestation and afforestation efforts.
- In five years, raise awareness and mobilize support for forest conservation by at least 50% of the community population by launching a campaign and network of forest defenders.

Candidate strategic goals: School board

- In five years, improve student achievement and outcomes

by implementing evidence-based curricula, assessments, and interventions across all grade levels and subjects.
- In five years, increase teacher retention and satisfaction by providing professional development, mentoring, feedback, recognition, and compensation opportunities.
- In five years, enhance parent and community engagement by establishing effective communication channels, partnerships, programs, and services.

Cause strategic goals: Anti-poverty

- In five years, increase the income of low-income households by providing financial education, counseling, coaching, and help.
- In five years, improve access and quality of basic services like health care, education, housing, food, and transportation for low-income households by pushing for policy changes and system reforms.
- In five years, enhance the voice and participation of low-income households in the community by building their leadership skills, confidence, networks, and opportunities. Tactics outline:

Outline Tactics and Actions

Continue to build your plan with the next layer of foundation and outline tactics or actions for each of your strategic goals. We will continue to refine and revise these tactical action plans in future chapters as well. These tactics should be concrete, realistic, and aligned with your resources and capacities.

Campaign tactics: Save the forests

- Support and collaborate with local communities and indigenous peoples who depend on the forests.
- Partner with local organizations and groups to plant trees and restore forests in selected areas.
- Educate and engage citizens and stakeholders on the benefits of forests and the importance of forest stewardship.
- Recruit and train volunteers and advocates who can spread the word and act for forest conservation in your community.

Candidate tactics: School board

- Establish clear and measurable goals for student achievement and quality instruction, and use data and evidence to track and evaluate their performance.
- Promote a culture of openness and teamwork with the superintendent, teachers, administrators, parents, students, and the community.
- School board members can use their power to push for policies and resources that align with their vision and goals.
- Network and build strong relationships with local organizations, businesses, institutions, and groups that can offer resources, services, programs, and opportunities for students, families, and schools.

Cause tactics: Anti-poverty

- Connect low-income households with financial resources like grants, scholarships, loans, subsidies, benefits, programs, and products to help them boost their income and assets.
- Lobby government officials and agencies to adopt and enforce policies and rules that better the access and quality of basic services for low-income households.

- Work with other organizations and groups that provide or push for basic services for low-income households.
- Organize events, activities, and forums, and create safe spaces for low-income households to share their stories, views, needs, and challenges.

Define Metrics for Success

Your plan is a roadmap that provides well-defined goals and objectives with clear deadlines to measure your success and adjust your course if needed. It's important to define how to measure success to achieve your goals, adjust your course if necessary, and celebrate victories.

Data-driven plans help capture the data to present to your team to understand progress, gaps, and needed improvements with metrics you use to measure your progress. You should track and compare them to your plan and roadmap to gain insights about your success and areas of improvement. A data-driven approach helps you build a strong foundation from startup up to scale and victory. Tracking and showcasing measures of success wins, and learning lessons help motivate your team and supporters.

Your plan is a living document. Be ready to adjust and make changes as necessary. There will always be challenges and constraints, and the best plans have a process to review and adjust dynamically so that you can adapt to changing circumstances and still find a path to victory.

Campaign metrics: Save the forests

- In five years, the number of trees planted in your community will increase by 250%.
- In five years, the level of awareness and support for forest

conservation in your community will increase by 50% by 2028.
- In five years, the number of volunteers and advocates for forest conservation will increase by 500% by 2028.

Candidate metrics: School board

- In five years, achieve at least 80% of stakeholder satisfaction with transparency and collaboration by 2028.
- In five years, the percentage of parents and community members who report high levels of satisfaction with the school district's communication, partnership, and engagement efforts will increase by 40% by 2028.
- In five years, the number of parents and community members who volunteer or donate to the school district will increase by 60% by 2028.

Cause metrics: Anti-poverty

- In five years, the number of low-income households that access and utilize financial education, counseling, coaching, and assistance will increase by 75% by 2028.
- In five years, the percentage of low-income households that report an improvement in their access and quality of basic services such as health care, education, housing, food, and transportation will increase by 30% by 2028.
- In five years, the percentage of low-income households that report an increase in their voice and participation in the community will increase by 35% by 2028.

 **Tip**

Create your plan with this template and samples to get started

1. **Vision statement:** Start with a vision statement that describes your desired future state in 3-5 years, based on the purpose statement that you created in Chapter 1. The vision statement should be clear, concise, and inspiring.

2. **Strategic goals:** Next, identify three strategic goals that will help you achieve your vision. These goals should be specific, measurable, achievable, relevant, and time-bound (SMART).

3. **Target audience:** Name the segments of the community, influencers, and partners to reach to achieve your goals and objectives.

4. **Tactics or actions:** Then, outline the tactics or actions that you will take to accomplish each goal. These tactics should be concrete, realistic, and aligned with your resources and capacities.

5. **Success metrics:** Finally, define the success metrics that you will use to evaluate your progress and impact. These metrics should be quantifiable, observable, and meaningful.

Here are a few examples of plans for a campaign, candidate, and cause.

Campaign: Protect the Environment

- **Goals**: Advocate for specific legislation to reduce fossil fuel influence and protect the environment. Raise awareness about how fossil fuels affect the environment.
- **Target Audience**: Environmental activists, legislators, and the public.
- **Strategy**: Use a mix of public awareness campaigns, lobbying efforts, and grassroots organizing to push for legislative change.
- **Tactics**: Organize rallies and public speaking events, launch an online campaign to raise awareness, and lobby legislators directly.
- **Team**: Recruit volunteers passionate about environmental issues. Assign roles based on skills and interests.
- **Measure outcomes:** Track legislation progress, measure the increase in public awareness (surveys, social media engagement), and monitor growth in the volunteer base.

Candidate for City Council

- **Goals**: Win the city council election. Advocate for policies that benefit residents.
- **Target audience:** Residents, and community leaders.
- **Strategy**: Connect with residents to understand their needs. Create policies that meet these needs.
- **Tactics:** Go door-to-door, hold town hall meetings, host community events, and engage on social media.
- **Team**: Find volunteers for door-to-door canvassing, organizing event organization, and managing social media.

- **Measure outcomes**: Track voter sentiment (polls/surveys), monitor election results, and measure social media engagement.

Cause to Address Hunger and Poverty

- **Goals**: Reduce hunger and poverty in the local community. Increase public awareness about these issues.
- **Target Audience**: Residents, businesses, and community leaders.
- **Strategy:** Organize food drives and fundraising events. Advocate for policies that address poverty.
- **Tactics**: Partner with local businesses for food drives, and fundraising, organize public awareness campaigns, lobby local leaders for policy change.
- **Team**: Recruit volunteers for event organization, fundraising, and lobbying efforts.
- **Measure outcomes**: Track the amount of food/money raised, measure the change in local poverty rates, and monitor policy changes.

★Success Story Profile: California Democratic Party Assembly Delegate Slate★

The California Democratic Party has a process for how Assembly District Delegates and Executive Board Representatives are selected in each of the 80 districts in California. Delegates to the State Party take part in important decisions including voting on endorsement recommendations and helping to promote the California Democratic Party's Platform and agenda. In 2017, the Assembly District

READY, SET, GO!

15 Progressive-Labor slate was formed with the vision, strategy, and plan to win.

- **Vision statement:** Our vision is to create a more accessible, grassroots, and progressive Democratic Party in Assembly District 15 that represents the values and needs of our diverse and vibrant community.

- **Strategic goals:** Elect the AD15 Progressive-Labor slate and candidate for Executive Board in the ADEM election on January 26, 2024. Build a coalition of grassroots support from progressive, labor, and diverse groups and secure endorsements from influential community leaders.

- **Target audience:** Eligible Democratic voters in AD15, especially those who are registered online or by mail, and those who are interested in progressive and labor issues. Strong supporters from various organizations and groups, such as unions, environmental groups, tenant rights groups, racial justice groups, and progressive political groups. Influential leaders and endorsers, such as elected officials, activists, celebrities, and experts, can vouch for our slate and candidate and persuade more voters to join us.

- **Tactics or actions:** Organize and mobilize at least 2000 eligible Democratic voters in AD15 to vote for our slate and candidate. Recruit and train at least 50 volunteers to help with our voting activities, like phone banking, text banking, canvassing, and social media outreach. Use email, texting, virtual phone banking, and social media to connect with voters and supporters, share our platform and bios, invite them to events, and remind them to vote. Seek endorsements from elected officials, influencers, and local groups that share our vision and values, such as Jovanka Beckles, Our Revolution East Bay, and other progressive and labor leaders. Showcase their endorsements on our website, social media, and materials. Create and distribute various materials to promote our slate and candidate, such as videos, printed slate cards, voter ballot cards, bios and platform flyers, candidate T-shirts, buttons, or stickers, canvassing signs, and scripts.

- **Success metrics:** Have at least 20 active volunteers who complete at least 4 hours of support activities each. Secure at least 10 endorsements from influential leaders and groups in our community. Achieve at least 80% voter turnout among our contact list of 2000+ voters. Win as many AD15 delegate seats as possible and elect our candidate for the Executive Board.

Test Your Plan

Testing your plan is a crucial step in the planning process, allowing you to evaluate your assumptions, identify strengths and weaknesses, and gather community feedback. Your plan is not fixed but a flexible strategy that needs to be tested throughout the planning process and during the implementation phase. Testing your plan will help you improve it, adapt it, and make it better.

- **Listen**: Conduct listening sessions with community members related to your goal. Share your draft plan and gather their insights.
- **Conduct surveys and polls**: Use online or phone surveys to collect data and feedback from a diverse audience.

- **Research**: Perform market research to understand the broader context of your operation.
- **Attend meetings**: If considering a local government role, attend city council or school board meetings to learn about the role and issues.
- **Meet with leaders**: Connect with community leaders for advice, guidance, and networking opportunities.
- **Host house parties**: Organize house parties to gather feedback, and find volunteers, donors, and advocates.
- **Understand priorities**: Gauge the priority level of your cause in your community to adjust your plan accordingly.

Chapter Checklist: Create Your Plan

Franklin's life is a testament to the power of planning and preparation. Whether he was contributing his wisdom and diplomatic skills to the drafting of the Declaration of Independence, establishing a new institution like the University of Pennsylvania, or serving as the first Postmaster General, a role crucial for reliable mail delivery, Franklin understood that success required a clear plan.

Your plan is a living document that should be flexible and adaptable to changes and challenges. It is your roadmap and guides you towards victory. By following the steps in this chapter, you now have a clear and effective plan to reach your goals. Just like Benjamin Franklin made a big impact through careful planning, you can make a significant difference in your community by following these steps. This highlights the importance of planning in any effort, including managing a campaign, running for office, or advocating for a cause. This chapter is meant to help you create a simple but effective plan and roadmap for your journey.

✓ **Checklist:**

1. You collaborated with your team to define clear roles and shared best practices.
2. You defined a strategy that aligns with your purpose and mission.
3. You set goals that are specific, measurable, achievable, rewarding, timely, inclusive, and equitable.
4. You applied power mapping and the theory of change to understand the power structures and dynamics affecting your issue or goal.
5. You outlined tactics and how they will help you achieve your outcomes.
6. You measured your success and tracked your progress using data and evidence.
7. You tested your plan and gathered feedback from your community through listening sessions, surveys, polls, and market research.

Step Two: SET

Climate change is the single biggest thing that humans have ever done on this planet. The one thing that needs to be bigger is our movement to stop it.

—Bill McKibben

Bill McKibben, an author, educator, environmentalist, and non-profit founder, brought the issue of climate change to the public more than three decades ago with his groundbreaking book, "The End of Nature." His relentless pursuit of environmental justice, from founding 350.org and the Third Act to leading the opposition against big oil pipeline projects, serves as a role model for aspiring activists.

The next steps of your journey to effect change, whether it's in your local community, on a national scale, or to save the planet, involve forming your team, preparing for action, and creating your message and platform.

- **Form your grassroots organization:** Recruit volunteers and supporters, define roles and responsibilities, and establish a communication plan. Spend time with your team to foster a positive organizational culture.

- **Run for office:** Identify the position you want to run for, understand the requirements and responsibilities, and prepare to launch your campaign. Whether you are running for local office or launching a new organization, this step is about putting your plan into action.

- **Create your message and platform:** Define your key messages based on your purpose and research. Develop a platform that addresses the needs of your community. Communicate your message effectively through various channels.

As you prepare to build your organization through meetings, rallies, and digital platforms, develop a calendar that includes different types of tactics needed, including events, endorsements, rallies, volunteer actions, and more. In the next chapters, you will form your organization, get set to launch your campaign or initiative and create your message and platform. It is about building a strong foundation for the work ahead.

Four

Form Your Organization

The greatest leaders are not those who seek power, but those who seek to empower others.

–Paul Wellstone

Paul Wellstone, an American academic, author, and politician, dedicated his life to championing progressive values and grassroots activism. From his early days as a professor at Carleton College in Minnesota to his tenure as a U.S. Senator representing Minnesota from 1991 until his tragic death in a plane crash in 2002, Wellstone was a tireless advocate for economic justice, healthcare reform, and environmental sustainability. His unique ability to rally students and community members around critical issues like poverty, education, and civil rights left an indelible mark on his community and the nation.

Throughout his life, Wellstone was committed to progressive values and a tireless advocate for economic justice, healthcare reform, and environmental sustainability. His ability to mobilize students and residents around issues such as poverty, education, and civil rights made him a beloved figure in his community. He developed the Wellstone Triangle as a framework to interconnect three leadership pillars: vision for public policy, community organizing, and electoral politics to create change. He believed that *"grassroots organizing is the opposite of big-money politics. It requires going directly to where people live and work, listening to their concerns, and building organizational structures that allow people to effectively be a voice for themselves."* Wellstone understood that finding, nurturing, and empowering new leaders was the way to build a sustainable movement for progressive change. Wellstone formed organizations that were not led by one or two people but embodied active and equal participation of their members since *"leadership is about how you bring out the best in other people."*

In this chapter, you will form your grassroots organization and empower all the leaders on your team. This involves building a team that is committed to your cause and creating an organizational structure that fosters collaboration, accessibility, inclusivity, and equitable communications. You will learn best practices and tips for creating structure, processes, and spaces to meet, collaborate, and form a sustainable organizational structure. Here are some of the areas you will explore:

- **Inspire leaders and build teams:** Learn why bringing people together for strong, reliable, and sustainable grassroots organizing is critical.
- **Create an inclusive environment:** Foster an environment that is accessible, inclusive, equitable, and just.
- **Define roles and responsibilities:** Learn how well-defined roles can help you collaborate effectively with your leadership team, members, supporters, and partner alliances.

Understand how to assign roles within your team based on individuals' skills and interests.

- **Document bylaws, roles, and rules:** Start with your purpose statement and create bylaws, roles, and rules with members of your leadership team with defined structures and decision-making processes.
- **Foster organizational culture, meetings, and communications:** Learn best practices for defining roles and responsibilities, organizing meetings, facilitating discussions, and setting up effective communication channels. Discover best practices for planning meetings that build trusted relationships. Learn how to keep everyone in your team informed and engaged.

Leadership Development and Team Building

Successful grassroots organizing relies on nurturing new leaders and fostering teamwork. It is about rallying people around a common cause and empowering them to make a difference. Without strong leadership and collaboration, grassroots efforts cannot thrive. Instead, inspire people to step into leadership roles and create a culture of teamwork for a strong, reliable, and sustainable grassroots organization for your campaign, candidate, or cause.

- Define your vision, mission, and goals.
- Develop your strategy and plan.
- Recruit and retain members and volunteers.
- Mobilize and engage your community.
- Communicate and collaborate effectively.
- Manage your resources and operations.
- Evaluate your progress and impact.

- Celebrate your successes and learn from your obstacles.

To cultivate leaders and build teams, you need to create a culture that fosters trust, respect, diversity, inclusion, and accountability. You also need to use strategies that help you identify, recruit, train, support, and retain potential leaders and team members.

It is important to create a robust, resilient, cohesive organization. A practical approach to do this is by organizing a planning workshop or retreat with your leadership team. Ideally, this event will be in person or will have a strong facilitator for a hybrid meeting if not all attendees can participate in person. A planning workshop or retreat can help you to:

- Build trust and rapport among your team members.
- Clarify roles and responsibilities.
- Identify strengths and weaknesses.
- Review goals and objectives.
- Develop a detailed action plan.
- Assign tasks and deadlines.
- Establish communication and feedback mechanisms.
- Celebrate and learn from each other.

To make the most of your planning workshop or retreat, you need to plan for before, during, and after the event, here are some tips to help you.

Before the event, send an invitation to save the date with a draft agenda at least two weeks in advance. Include the purpose, objectives, location, date, time, duration, and expected outcomes of the event. Ask your team members to complete some assignments in advance to prepare for the meeting. For example, you can ask them to do a SWOT (strengths, weaknesses, opportunities, and threats) analysis of your campaign, candidate, or cause; to research best practices or case studies from similar campaigns; or to brainstorm ideas for fundraising, outreach, or media strategies. Plan the meeting with help from people with strong facilitation skills. They can help you design and run the activities, keep the discussion focused and productive, manage conflicts and disagreements, and ensure that everyone has a chance to participate and contribute.

During the event, start with an icebreaker activity to warm up the group and break the ice. This can be a fun game, a personal introduction, or a shared experience. Establish ground rules or community norms for the meeting. For example, you can ask your team members to respect each other's opinions, listen actively, speak one at a time, stay on topic, and be constructive and supportive. Outline the roles and duties of each team member for the meeting. For instance, designate someone as the facilitator (who guides the process), the recorder (who takes notes), the timekeeper (who keeps track of time), and the energizer (who uplifts the team's spirit). Use a range of methods and tools to engage your team members and spark their creativity. This could include brainstorming sessions (where everyone generates as many ideas as possible without judgment), affinity diagrams (where similar ideas are grouped into categories), prioritization matrices (where ideas are ranked based on criteria), and action plans (where the steps, resources, responsibilities, and deadlines for each idea are outlined). Take breaks regularly to refresh your mind and body. You can also incorporate some physical activities or games to keep your team members energized and motivated. Conclude the meeting with a summary of the key points and outcomes. Encourage team members to provide feedback on what worked well and areas for improvement. Express gratitude for their participation and dedication. Thank them for their participation and commitment.

After the event, follow up as soon as possible with all attendees. Send them a summary report of the meeting that includes the notes, action items, next steps, draft documents, photos, and videos if appropriate to capture the people and creative energy in the event. Keep track of your action plan's progress and regularly touch base with your team members. Offer them the support, guidance, and recognition they need as they accomplish their tasks. Plan for annual retreats as part of your ongoing planning process. This will help you review your achievements, challenges, and lessons learned; adjust your objectives, strategies, and tactics; and renew your enthusiasm, passion, and vision.

 Tip

> A leadership culture is one where everyone feels valued, empowered, and welcomed to contribute to the organization's objectives. It is also a place where everyone has the chance to hone their leadership abilities and potential. To create a culture of leadership, you can:
>
> 1. **Communicate:** Share your vision, mission, and goals with your team, and welcome their thoughts and feedback.
>
> 2. **Create teams:** Foster a sense of participation and teamwork and offer opportunities for leadership roles or tasks.
>
> 3. **Train:** Equip your team with training and coaching to boost their leadership skills and confidence.

4. **Lead by example:** Model values and behaviors such as integrity, honesty, respect, and commitment.

5. **Recognize:** appreciate their efforts and achievements and celebrate their victories.

Many organizations offer training and resources to help you get started, drawing from best practices. This next success story profile illustrates this best practice.

★Success Story Profile: Indivisible★

Indivisible is a national grassroots movement that was formed to resist the Trump agenda and hold elected officials accountable. It started as a guide written by former congressional staffers, who shared their insider knowledge on how to influence members of Congress through local advocacy. The guide went viral and inspired thousands of people across the country to form local groups and take action.

Indivisible provides these groups with resources, tools, and support, promoting principles reflecting values of inclusion, tolerance, and fairness. It also helps groups coordinate national campaigns to put pressure on their representatives and senators. Local groups pressure elected officials through actions like attending town halls, making phone calls, staging rallies, or writing letters. It exemplifies how everyday people can transform into inspiring leaders and build effective teams for grassroots organizing.

A primary goal of Indivisible is to empower ordinary citizens to become leaders and organizers within their communities. It offers resources, tools, and support for those wishing to start or join a local group and connect with other groups in their area or state. It also encourages groups to adopt principles reflecting values of inclusion, tolerance, and fairness. Here are the steps to form a local group:

- **Start a local group:** This could be a subgroup of an existing activist group or a new effort. The most important thing is that the group is focused on applying local pressure to Members of Congress.
- **Recruit co-founders:** Find a few people who are interested in participating and recruiting others. Include people with diverse social networks to maximize your group's reach. Strive to ensure that the leadership reflects the diversity of the community.
- **Email contacts and post on social media:** Reach out to potential members through email and social media: Extend invitations to join the group by sending emails and posting messages on various platforms. Explain the purpose and goals of the group and ask people to sign up.
- **Invite everyone to a kickoff meeting:** Use this meeting to agree on a name, principles, roles, communication methods, and strategy for the group. Keep the meeting focused on the core strategy of applying pressure to the members of Congress. Share ideas and feedback and encourage participation and collaboration.
- **Enlist people to recruit across their networks:** Ask every member to send out outreach emails or posts to their contacts. Recruit people for the email list and aim for many members. Make a conscious effort to diversify the group and center around the communities most affected by the Trump agenda.

By following these steps, anyone can form a local group join the movement, and make an impact through actions, such as attending town halls, making phone calls, staging rallies, or writing letters. These groups demonstrate how ordinary people can become inspiring leaders and build effective teams for grassroots organizing.

 Tip

You can follow these steps to start a non-profit progressive group from scratch.

1. **Organize:** Bring together a group of progressive people in your community who share your progressive values and goals. Reach out to people, organizations, and communities early on to involve them in the formation of your group. Set up a meeting time and place to discuss your vision and plans.

2. **Write bylaws:** These are the basic rules that your group will agree to follow. Have a small team draft the bylaws, then propose them to the larger group for feedback and amendments. Vote to approve the bylaws.

3. **Meet regularly:** It is helpful to have a consistent rhythm for your meetings. For example, you can have general membership meetings once a month, and executive board meetings in between.

4. **Create community guidelines:** It is important to foster

a welcoming and respectful environment where everyone's voice matters and where individuals can learn and grow. Create community guidelines to be read at the start of each meeting, reinforcing the kind of space you want to create.

5. **Reach out:** Outreach is important to build your membership and support base. You can set up booths at local farmers markets, festivals, events, and college campuses. Also, show up and support other organizations and movements that focus on specific issues, such as police violence, immigrant rights, and environmental justice. This shows your commitment to the broader movement and helps build trust within the community.

6. **Apply to be an affiliate of a national organization:** If you want to join a larger network of progressive groups, you can apply to be an affiliate of a national organization that shares your values and goals.

7. **File as an organization:** You will need to choose a legal status for your group.

By following these steps, you are on your way to forming a grassroots group that can make a difference in your community. Next, review another success story profile that showcases this process in action.

★Success Story Profile: San Francisco Berniecrats ★

San Francisco Berniecrats is a local grassroots group of Our Revolution. The group was formed in 2016 after the Bernie Sanders presidential campaign to continue the goals of the campaign and to build the movement. They are focused on local grassroots organizing because change begins locally. The group operates democratically, with major decisions and endorsements made through a vote of its membership.

San Francisco Berniecrats has a clear and effective organizational structure that defines the roles, rules, and responsibilities of its members and participants. The group has adopted a set of bylaws that outline the name, purpose, limitations, officers, membership, meetings, committees, voting, and amending procedures of the group. The group has established community guidelines that foster a welcoming and respectful atmosphere for all. It is led by four officers: a Chairperson, a Co-Chairperson, a Secretary, and a Treasurer, who are elected by the members for two-year terms. Additionally, the group operates through various committees and working groups that handle functions and activities such as social media, curriculum development, advocacy, fundraising, and outreach.

San Francisco Berniecrats meets regularly to discuss and decide on various matters related to its purpose and goals. The group actively engages in outreach and recruitment to expand its membership and support base. It stands as an ally to other organizations and movements that align with its vision of a more equitable and inclusive society.

San Francisco Berniecrats is an example of how ordinary people can become inspiring leaders and build effective teams for grassroots organizing. The group shows how to establish an organizational structure that promotes coordination, communication, delegation, accountability, transparency, and alignment. It also showcases how to foster an inclusive environment that encourages a sense of belonging, respect, and empowerment. Furthermore, it demonstrates how to effect positive social change that benefits everyone.

Create an Inclusive Environment

Creating an inclusive environment is very important. Organize a space that is accessible, inclusive, equitable, and just for everyone, particularly for anyone who has been historically marginalized or oppressed. This environment promotes a sense of belonging, respect, and empowerment among all members and participants of the organization or movement.

- **Organize**: Create a space that is accessible, inclusive, equitable, and just, promoting a sense of belonging, respect, and empowerment among all members.
- **Conduct outreach**: Target diverse groups and communities in your area for recruitment activities. Use various platforms and methods to connect with potential members and supporters.
- **Foster dialogue**: Create a safe and supportive space for interaction among your members. Set ground rules and norms that encourage mutual respect, trust, and understanding.
- **Offer training**: Provide diversity, equity, and inclusion training to your members. Assist them in developing the necessary awareness, knowledge, and skills to recognize and challenge bias, discrimination, and oppression.
- **Embrace diversity**: Appreciate the diversity and contributions of your members. Acknowledge the unique strengths,

talents, and perspectives each person brings to the organization.
- **Promote equity**: Ensure everyone has equal access to opportunities, resources, and decision-making processes within your organization. Advocate for rules that meet the needs of everyone in your community.

By doing this, you will make your grassroots efforts stronger and more sustainable. You will build a diverse team that can reach your goals, connect better with your community, and gain more support. Most importantly, you will make a positive change that benefits everyone.

★Success Story Profile: National Equity Project★

The National Equity Project is an organization that helps leaders and teams change their systems into equitable, resilient, and liberating environments. They work with schools, organizations, and communities to help people create educated, just societies where everyone thrives. Their mission is to transform the experiences, outcomes, and life options for children and families who have been historically underserved by our institutions and systems.

The National Equity Project provides programs customized to support leaders in their equity journey. They offer consulting and coaching to help leaders and teams make informed decisions and take more effective action. They design and facilitate professional learning experiences for educators and other leaders to reimagine and redesign their systems for equity. They also create and share tools and resources to catalyze new thinking and transform action in schools, organizations, and communities.

The National Equity Project is guided by a set of beliefs that inform their work. They believe that it is possible to achieve more just, equitable, and liberating systems by acknowledging and addressing the historical and ongoing impacts of racism and white supremacy. They believe that the current systems perpetuate inequity by design and that new, liberating systems must be designed with conscious intention and a shared vision. They believe that we need one another and that our fates are linked. They believe that listening, sharing stories, healing, and deepening relationships foster genuine belonging.

Roles, Rules, and Bylaws

As you form your grassroots organization it is important to bring together your leadership team to finalize your leadership structure with roles, rules, and bylaws for decision-making and communications processes for your team. It is important to take the time to set up the foundation for the culture of your team including the values, community agreements, and communications to bring people together for a strong, reliable, and sustainable grassroots organization. A well-defined organizational structure can help you:

- Coordinate and communicate better among your members and participants.
- Delegate and distribute tasks and resources efficiently and fairly.
- Avoid or resolve conflicts and misunderstandings.
- Enhance accountability and transparency.
- Align your actions with your vision, mission, and goals.

Set up the roles for your grassroots group so it can operate smoothly and effectively.

- **Chair**: Ensures the group follows its rules and respects all members. Leads meetings, sends out the agenda, handles outside communication, and is easily contactable.
- **Co-Chair**: Shares the role or steps in if the Chairperson cannot serve.
- **Secretary**: Drafts clear and accurate minutes of all meetings and maintains an archived digital copy of minutes, bylaws, and other relevant documents.
- **Treasurer**: Manages all financial transactions, keeps track of all money, prepares and presents financial reports at meetings and upon request.
- **Membership**: Open to anyone who supports the group's goals. Members can vote, run for office, join in meetings and activities, and use the group's information and resources.
- **Meetings**: Regular meetings are held at least once every two months. Officers decide when and where these meetings will happen and provide at least two weeks' notice of each meeting to the members.
- **Committees and Working Groups**: Officers can create committees or working groups if needed. The leader of each group will update everyone on their work at meetings and when asked.
- **Voting**: Voting on any matter shall be by a show of hands or by secret ballot if requested by any member. A majority vote of the members who are present at a meeting where there is a quorum shall decide any matter.
- **Amending Bylaws**: To change these rules, two-thirds of the members at a meeting need to agree. This can only happen if the proposed change is shared with the members at least two weeks before the meeting.

 **Tip**

You can create an organizational structure by adopting a set of bylaws that outline the basic rules and roles of your organization. Bylaws are a written document that specifies the name, purpose, officers, membership, meetings, committees, voting, and amending procedures of your organization or movement. Bylaws can help you establish a formal and legal framework for your organization or movement, as well as provide guidance and clarity for your members and participants.

1. **Name:** The name of your organization or movement

2. **Purpose:** The general and specific purposes of your organization or movement

3. **Officers:** The roles, terms, election, and duties of the officers of your organization or movement

4. **Membership:** The criteria, rights, and responsibilities of the members of your organization or movement

5. **Meetings:** The frequency, notice, agenda, quorum, and minutes of the meetings of your organization or movement

6. **Committees and working groups:** The formation, composition, and functions of the committees and working groups of your organization or movement.

> 7. **Voting:** The procedures and requirements for voting on various matters by your organization or movement
>
> 8. **Amending bylaws:** The procedures and requirements for amending the bylaws of your organization or movement

You will need to decide if your group will be run by volunteers only, or a mix of volunteers and staff. This decision will depend on your goals, resources, and plans for your current and future state, and the availability of support from a national or regional organization. Here are some points to keep in mind:

- Some groups can be run just by volunteers, especially if they're part of a bigger organization that gives them resources and tools. This can save money and time, and make the volunteers feel more involved.
- But some groups might need staff, especially if they have big goals, complicated tasks, or a lot of work to do. Staff can bring skills, keep things running smoothly, and help with things like fundraising, digital, writing grants, and administrative tasks.
- Planning for staff, places to work, and other big, long-term things need careful thought and decision-making. It can be hard to hire staff until you have the basics of your group set up, like what your mission is, what your rules are, and what your budget is. You also need to think about the legal and financial side of having staff, like taxes, payroll, and benefits.
- Sometimes, you can hire contractors, consultants, or local experts who can give your group-specific services or skills. This

can be more flexible and cheaper than hiring staff. However, you still need to have clear agreements and expectations with them and monitor their performance and quality.

As you work to build out your organizational strategy and structure, it is important to name these decisions in your goals and planning structures. You should also consult with your core team, your members, and your allies to get their input and feedback on these decisions.

Culture, Meetings, and Communications

During this time, it is very important to spend time with the people who are part of your team. Lead by example to establish the organizational culture. Create a structure for meetings (in person, online), and set up a directory and communications.

 Tip

> Managing your team effectively is crucial for ensuring that your organization runs smoothly and efficiently. It also helps you avoid or resolve any problems or challenges that may affect your team's performance or morale. To manage your team effectively, you can:
>
> 1. **Set expectations:** Set clear goals for your team members.
>
> 2. **Delegate:** Delegate tasks according to the skills, interests, and availability of your team members.

3. **Provide feedback:** Schedule regular feedback on the progress of tasks.

4. **Support:** Provide support or assistance when needed by team members.

5. **Address concerns:** Resolve any issues or conflicts among team members in a fair manner.

6. **Review:** Evaluate the results of tasks done by team members.

By following these tips, you can inspire leaders and build teams that will help you achieve your grassroots organizing goals. Leadership is not about having authority or power over others but about empowering others to lead themselves. Teamwork is not about working alone but about working together towards a common vision.

 Tip

Creating a strong mission statement is crucial for defining your organization's purpose and goals. Here are some steps to guide you:

1. **Define what you do:** Clearly state the primary activities or services your organization provides.

> 2. **Identify your audience:** Specify who benefits from your services or activities.
>
> 3. **Explain how you do it:** Describe the unique methods or approaches your organization uses to deliver its services.
>
> 4. **Highlight the benefits:** Explain how your services or activities help your audience.

A well-crafted mission statement can effectively communicate your organization's purpose and drive its success. To help shape your mission statement, consider these questions:

- Why did you start your organization?
- What do you want your organization to be known for?
- Who do you need to serve?
- How will your work benefit your community?
- What core values or beliefs guide your work?
- What is missing in your community that your organization can provide?
- How will you measure success?

Community Agreements and Norms

When you are starting your grassroots group, it is a good idea to make a list of a set of community agreements or norms that show you value respect, safety, honesty, and thoughtfulness. These rules can guide how your team members treat each other and the wider community. They help foster a culture where diverse backgrounds and perspectives are valued, and where everyone is united by their commitment to the purpose, mission, and values.

Community agreements are the rules you agree with your organization. They guide how you behave, communicate, and make decisions. They can also help you build a team culture that is welcoming and fair to everyone.

It is important that everyone feels safe and respected. Any kind of harassment will not be allowed. The team should practice stepping up and stepping back to ensure that all members can share their voices. For example, if you have not spoken much, try to share your thoughts and opinions. You can ask questions, give feedback, or show support for others. Your voice is important and can make the discussion better. And, if you have spoken a lot or dominated the conversation, step back and make space for others to speak. You can also invite others to share their views, acknowledge their contributions, or listen actively and respectfully. Your silence can create room for others to grow and learn.

 Tip

> Creating community agreements and norm statements is a crucial part of fostering a respectful and productive team environment. These agreements set the tone for how team members interact with each other and help to create a culture of mutual respect and understanding. Here are some tips for creating effective community agreements and norm statements:
>
> 1. **Be specific**: Norms should be specific, observable, and measurable. For example, instead of saying "We treat

each other with respect", say "We show respect by listening attentively and not interrupting each other".

2. **Involve everyone**: Norms should be created by consensus, not by decree. Everyone on the team should have a voice and a vote in deciding what norms to adopt. This way, the team members will feel more committed and accountable to follow them.

3. **Review regularly**: Norms are not set in stone. They should be revisited regularly and updated as needed. The team should also monitor and evaluate how well they are following the norms and address any issues or violations.

4. **Be consistent**: Norms are only effective if they are followed consistently. The team leader and the team members should remind each other of the norms and hold each other accountable for adhering to them.

Community agreements are co-created by the members of a community and reflect their values, expectations, and needs. Some examples of community agreements or norms are:

- **Be present and engaged:** Participate actively, listen attentively, and share your thoughts and feelings.
- **Respect diversity and differences:** Appreciate and celebrate the diversity of identities, backgrounds, and perspectives in the community. Be open-minded and respectful of others' opinions and experiences.
- **Communicate constructively:** Use positive and supportive

language, avoid personal attacks and judgments, and give constructive feedback. Seek to understand before being understood.
- **Respect privacy:** Keep other people's personal or sensitive information private, and do not share it without their permission. Make sure the community is a safe and trusting place.
- **Keep learning:** Be open to learning from others, question your own beliefs and assumptions, and be brave enough to take risks. Embrace mistakes as opportunities for growth.

Here is a sample community agreement statement:

"*As members of this team, we commit to fostering a culture that prioritizes respect, safety, good faith, and thoughtfulness always. We agree to treat one another with respect by listening attentively and not interrupting each other. We will work together to find equitable solutions to any issues that may arise. We will practice stepping up and stepping back to ensure that all voices are heard. We understand that the way we respond matters, and we will always respect the person with whom we're communicating. We will always use language consistent with our values.*"

★*Success Story Profile: Chapter Digital Strategies*★

The Chapter Digital Strategies team created this community agreement with the Sierra Club Chapters, Groups, and volunteer leaders.

"Digital Community Standards

Thank you for being a part of the Sierra Club digital community! We are excited to welcome you to this dynamic, collaborative, and growing digital learning journey. We are more powerful together when we are aligned in shared values, norms, and processes. We believe that engaging in a safe and trusted community empowers us to build clear pathways to digital learning focused on roles, resources, and clear expectations so that we may gain a better understanding of how we can help support your needs. To ensure a spirit of constructive collaboration across the digital user community, we require mutual commitments to:

- A kind, conscious, and respectful working environment for all.
- An attitude of cooperation, open-minded curiosity, and willingness to learn new things.
- Accountability to Sierra Club's mission, values, and standards of conduct.
- Adherence to all policies for the appropriate use of Sierra Club's digital systems and data."

Create Your Nonprofit Organization

Once you have formed your core leadership team it is important to decide what type of organization you want to create.

- Choose your nonprofit name.
- Set up a board of directors.
- File incorporation documents.
- Create bylaws and operating rules.
- Get an employer identification number (EIN).

 Tip

Starting a local political club in your community, regardless of political affiliation, involves several key steps. Here's a generic process that you can follow:

1. **Recruit your core leadership team:** Reach out to people in your community who share your political views and might be interested in helping you start a club.

2. **Review guidelines:** Check the guidelines of your state and county party organization for starting a new club. This will help you understand the process, rules, and deadlines.

3. **Draft bylaws:** Draft the bylaws for your new club based on the requirements of your party organization. These bylaws will govern how your club operates.

4. **Schedule an organizing meeting:** Schedule a formal organizing meeting for the new club. This meeting should be well-prepared and start and end on time.

5. **Define your geographic focus:** Decide on the geographic focus of your club. This could be within a city's borders, or it could include nearby towns, depending on the size of your community.

6. **Establish regular meetings:** Schedule regular meetings for your club members. Aim to have at least nine general meetings a year.

7. **Elect officers:** Conduct elections for club officers as per the process outlined in your bylaws.

8. **Request a charter:** Once your club is established, request a charter from your party organization. This will give your club official recognition.

9. **Register your club:** Request an Employer Identification Number (EIN) from the IRS and file with the Secretary of State. This will allow you to open a bank account for the club, fundraise, and carry out expenditures while following the law.

★Success Story Profile: California Democratic Council★

The California Democratic Council serves Democratic Clubs and Central Committees in California. It provides these entities with a voice at the state level, fostering a relationship based on grassroots energy, leadership, passion, collaboration, and integrity. It operates as a network, offering a variety of resources and services to ensure Democratic Clubs can effectively serve all California Democrats. It advocates for all clubs and central committees, giving them a platform to voice their concerns and interests at the state level. It assists affiliated Democratic Clubs and Central Committees in the development and advocacy of platform items and resolutions. It also aids in organizational growth through training, skill-building, intra-club collaboration, and candidate development. The CDC's mission is to empower Democratic entities across California, fostering a more robust and inclusive political landscape.

Starting a New Democratic Club So you want to start a club? Let us help you by sharing both our expertise and resources. A brief overview of the process:

1. Identify and contact local Democrats from your community who you think may be interested in helping you start a club.

2. Find the bylaws for your Democratic County Central Committee on their website or by contacting a member of the board. Check for chartering requirements and draft your bylaws. Sample bylaws can be found below.

3. Schedule a formal organizing meeting for the new Club. A restaurant or someone's house works well for the first meeting. The first official meeting should be very well prepared and should start on time and end on time. Print the first agenda in advance, and include a) the adoption of geographic focus, b) the adoption of bylaws, c) the officer election process, and d) choosing the next meetings.

4. At the first meeting, after introductions, let the group know one of the first challenges for any Democratic club is to agree on the geographic focus. Pass a vote on your focus as the first item. Sometimes it makes sense for a municipal club to focus on organizing Democrats within a city's borders. Other times, especially for small towns under 2,000 residents, it may make sense to partner with Democrats in nearby towns to establish a local club.

5. CDC believes a viable local club should schedule at least nine general meetings a year and should aim for a minimum club membership of three percent (3%) of the registered Democrats in its boundaries.

6. Distribute draft bylaws to the new club members if you did not distribute them in your meeting announcement. After the adoption of by-laws, the next order of business is the

election process. Be sure to schedule your next meetings before you adjourn.

7. Now that you're a club, the next step will be to request a charter from your Democratic County Central Committee. The benefits of chartering vary by club but usually include a voice and vote on the Committee, the ability to present resolutions and funding requests, and access to other resources. Contact the board of your Democratic County Central Committee to request approval for your charter.

8. Once your charter gets approved, you will need to get an EIN from the IRS and register with the Secretary of State. This will let you open a bank account for the club, raise money, and spend money while following the law. Congratulations, you are now a club!

Chapter Checklist: Form Your Organization

As Paul Wellstone, a beacon of progressive values and grassroots activism, once said, "The greatest leaders are not those who seek power, but those who seek to empower others." This sentiment is at the heart of forming an effective grassroots organization. It is about creating a culture where everyone works together and feels included and empowered to contribute to the cause.

In this chapter, you learned how to start your grassroots organization, a group of people who share your values and goals and work together to achieve them. You learned how to engage with your team, decide who does what, make a mission statement and rules, and set up a communication plan. You also learned how to create an organizational culture that fosters democracy, diversity, and empowerment.

This chapter is inspired by the organizing philosophy of Paul Wellstone, a former senator and progressive leader who said: "It is not enough to inspire people with vision and good public policy." He knew that to make a difference in society, you need a group of people ready to stand up for it. This group grows through grassroots organizing. Grassroots organizing is the opposite of politics controlled by big money. It requires going directly to where people live and work, listening to their concerns, and building organizational structures that allow people to effectively be a voice for themselves. It is ongoing work that does not come and go with election cycles. It is rooted in long-term relationships.

Starting your grassroots group is not just about setting up the structure of your group. It is also about ensuring each member can effectively advocate for your cause. By following these steps, you're on your way to creating a strong, lasting group that can effectively stand up for your cause.

 Checklist:

1. You formed your organization by meeting with your leadership team and establishing norms and guidelines for collaboration.
2. You fostered a safe and productive environment that is accessible, inclusive, equitable, and just.
3. You assigned roles within your team based on your leader's skills and interests.
4. You used your mission statement and purpose to identify core members for your leadership team and define key structures and decision-making processes.
5. You defined roles, ran effective meetings, guided discussions, and set up efficient communication methods.

Five

Run for Office

If they don't give you a seat at the table, bring a folding chair.

−Shirley Chisholm

Picture in your mind, Shirley Chisholm, the first African-American woman elected to Congress in 1968. She dared to run for a redistricted New York congressional seat without the support of the Brooklyn Democratic Party bosses. She positioned herself as *"the people's politician,"* advocating for higher wages for workers, increased funding for public education, and respect for black Americans and women. Upon arriving on Capitol Hill, she disrupted institutional norms, carving out spaces that had previously been reserved for white men. She navigated the political landscape by following her playbook, earning both friends and foes on both sides of the aisle.

As you embark on your journey to run for office, let Shirley Chisholm's story inspire you. Like her, you may face obstacles and opposition. But remember her motto is *"unbought and unbossed."* Stand up for what you think is right, challenge the status quo, and represent the people who trust you. Shirley Chisholm's powerful message, *"If they don't give you a seat at the table, bring a folding chair,"* is a rallying cry for all grassroots progressive candidates. It embodies the spirit of resilience, determination, and the willingness to challenge the status quo.

For grassroots candidates, this message is particularly significant. Likely, you are not part of the political establishment with deep financial pockets, and insider connections. You may lack the traditional backing or resources that established politicians have. You have something powerful: a strong bond with your community and a promise to represent their interests.

Running for office might seem scary. You might think you need a law degree, big money donors, years of political experience, or to be famous. But what you need is to care about others, want to make things better, work well with others, and know that you are enough.

Chisholm's message encourages progressive grassroots candidates to create opportunities rather than waiting for them to be handed down. It is a story about having the strength and audacity to take on the political establishment, create meaningful change, and make your voice heard. Chisholm's words remind us that even when things are tough and the odds are against us, we can still make a difference. They highlight how important it is to represent others and to stand up for what we believe in. So, as you get ready to run for office, don't worry about what you think you need. Instead, focus on what you already have: your passion, your values, and your vision for a better future. Be unbought, unbossed, and unafraid to bring your folding chair. Fight for what you believe in, even when things get tough. The ability to make a difference doesn't come from what you have, but from how determined you are to fight for your cause.

This chapter will help guide you through the steps of running for office. You will explore various elected and nominated positions in your desired district, assess your readiness and fit, and prepare the resources, support, and strategy needed to win your race.

- **Understand the political landscape**: Running for office is an opportunity to dive into democracy. You need to align your passion and purpose with available opportunities and ensure you are a good fit for the position.
- **Balance commitments:** Running for office can be a full-time job. You'll need to balance this commitment with your existing responsibilities and understand what serving in the position entails.
- **Navigate election requirements**: Familiarize yourself with the rules, timelines, and schedules specific to the office you're running for. Whether it is a general election or primary, partisan, or nonpartisan race, understanding these details will help you navigate your political journey.
- **Prepare for victory**: Winning an election requires effort, lots of it. You will need to assemble a team to investigate fundraising and voter outreach strategies before filing your candidacy. Learn how to plan your public announcement, build your volunteer base, start your fundraising campaign, and identify target voter strategies.

By the end of this chapter, you will have found the office you want to run for, assessed your fit, assembled your campaign committee, and prepared to launch your campaign. You will be ready to put your name on the ballot and take your first steps towards victory.

Understand the Political Landscape

There are many ways to get involved in politics. You can pass resolutions, lobby for issues, help with voting, volunteer, or work for candidate campaigns, serve at the polls, run for delegate positions in political parties and organizations, and even run for office. With over 500,000 elected positions in the U.S. and many more opportunities to serve in nominated positions and volunteer roles, it is important to find the right fit for you.

The world of politics in the U.S. has historically been dominated by older, white men. But recently, there has been a change towards more diverse representation. Candidates of all ages, genders, races, and backgrounds are running for office, challenging the way things are and bringing new ideas to leadership roles.

This change is happening at all levels of government, local, state, and federal. Diverse candidates are not just running, but winning, changing the power dynamics towards a more inclusive and democratic representation in our communities. These pioneers are setting new standards and serving as role models for future generations of leaders. Their victories show that leadership comes in many forms and that our elected officials should truly represent the diverse communities they serve. This trend towards increased diversity in political leadership is a positive step towards a more inclusive and representative democracy. It has shifted the image of the elected official across many jurisdictions.

Running for office is a big decision and commitment with so much opportunity to make a positive and powerful impact in your community, especially in state and local level jurisdictions across municipalities, and counties. There are thousands of elections happening every year. Take some time to read, think, and learn about the opportunities and where you might fit in to make a difference.

- **Local:** Positions include mayor, city or town council members, county commissioners, planning and zoning commissioners, school boards, coroners, and sheriffs.
- **State:** There are agencies, boards and commissions, executive branch offices including the Governor, Secretary of State, Treasurer, Attorney General, legislative branch Senators and Representatives, and committees, and judicial branch courts and judges.
- **Federal:** There are 542 federal offices. These include the President, Vice President, 100 U.S. Senators (two from each state), 435 U.S. Representatives, four delegates to the House of Representatives from U.S. territories and the District of Columbia, and one Resident Commissioner from the Commonwealth of Puerto Rico.

City council: Being a part of your local town or city council is a wonderful way to represent your community. This role allows you to act as a lawmaker for your local area. Once elected, you will have the power to review and approve budgets, vote to pass ordinances, resolutions, and regulations, establish taxes, regulate land zones through zoning laws, and represent your community at the state and federal levels.

Mayor: A mayor is the chief executive of a city, responsible for managing and preparing the city budget, overseeing daily operations, appointing advisory boards or commissions, enforcing legislation, and more. A mayor supervises the city's main departments, such as police, fire, education, housing, health, and sanitation, and often appoints their heads. A mayor also has final authority over fiscal issues and budgetary concerns.

City Manager: The city manager, hired by the city council, implements policies, oversees operations, and manages the budget and personnel. Their interaction with the city council and mayor varies by the form of municipal government.

School Board: A school board is a group of elected individuals shaping the functioning of community schools. They make decisions about school rules, budgets, programs, resources, curriculum, and staff. They also ensure all students receive a fair, inclusive, and high-quality education.

Board of Supervisors: This team of elected individuals manages county operations. They handle the budget, taxes, and ordinances, and represent county issues at the state and federal levels. They also play a key role in voter registration, and elections, and sometimes manage state-required social services programs.

County Clerk: A county clerk maintains records related to a county's population, including vital records, licenses, permits, deeds, titles, elections, and voter registration. They also serve customers, handle inquiries, and perform administrative tasks. Their role ensures the county's records are accurate, accessible, and secure.

★Success Story Profile: Catherine McMullen★

Catherine McMullen is the County Clerk for Clackamas County, chosen by voters in November 2022. She has more than 17 years of experience in public service, starting her career as a public librarian. She is dedicated to making sure everyone has fair and equal access to voting and that elections in Clackamas County are correct, safe, and open.

Catherine McMullen defeated Sherry Hall who was the Clackamas County Clerk for 20 years. Hall faced several controversies and scandals during her tenure, including ballot misprints, voter pamphlet errors, delayed results, and budget overruns. She was widely criticized for her lack of accountability, transparency, and competence in managing the county's elections. She also lost the trust and confidence of the public and the county officials, who repeatedly offered her help and oversight.

Catherine McMullen ran against Hall with a message of election integrity and competency, promising to improve the quality and efficiency of the county's elections. She also pledged to increase staffing, implement quality control measures, and ensure equitable and fair access to the ballot. She won the election with almost twice as many votes as Hall and became the new County Clerk in 2022.

As County Clerk, Catherine McMullen prioritizes improving her office's services and functions. She ensures timely, accurate election results and addresses ballot security concerns. She provides an opt-in ballot tracking service and focuses on increasing voter participation, especially among historically ignored voters. She also establishes emergency processes for ballot distribution during crises.

McMullen collaborates with community leaders and stakeholders to empower Clackamas County's diverse communities. She ensures public records are easily accessible and implements sound records management practices. She strives to remove racist language from covenants and deeds. She processes passport applications and issues marriage licenses impartially and conducts weddings for all residents, including same-sex couples.

District Attorney: A district attorney, or DA, is a person who works for the state to handle criminal cases in a specific area. They work with police to investigate crimes, decide what charges to bring, and take those cases to court. But their job isn't just in the courtroom. They also help make laws about crime, advise lawmakers, and help people understand important issues. The DA's commitment to protecting victims' rights, prosecuting criminals, and deterring crime fosters a sense of security within the community. Their role is integral to maintaining a fair and just society, holding individuals accountable for their actions, and ensuring justice is served for all.

★Success Story Profile: Pamela Price★

Pamela Price, elected as the Alameda County District Attorney in 2022, has dedicated her life to justice. Her experiences with sexual harassment, domestic violence, and the criminal justice system have shaped her commitment.

Price started her legal career as a defense attorney in San Francisco, often representing young people involved in the criminal justice system. Over the next three decades, she became a well-known civil rights attorney, helping many victims of retaliation, wrongful termination, and discrimination.

Price is committed to changing the criminal justice system and reducing racial disparity in prosecutions. In 2002, she was one of the few Black women to argue before the U.S. Supreme Court. She successfully represented her client, Abner Morgan, a Black electrician who faced constant racial harassment at work. Their victory established the "continuing violation" doctrine that applies to all discrimination cases brought under federal law in the U.S., earning Price the California Lawyer of the Year in Employment (CLAY) Award. Price's activism extends beyond the courtroom. She has been a leader in several groups, including the Bay Area Defense Committee for Battered Women, the National Conference of Black Lawyers, and the Lawyers Committee for Civil Rights in San Francisco. In 2016, she was elected to the Alameda County Democratic Central Committee, where she pushed for her community and sponsored resolutions for progressive change. Her hard work and service to Alameda County led to her being named Woman of the Year for Assembly District 18 by Assemblymember Rob Bonta and the California Legislative Women's Caucus in 2017. Price's story is one of relentless dedication to justice and community service, demonstrating that with passion and commitment, it is possible to effect meaningful change.

Congress: Congressional representatives play a pivotal role in shaping the nation's laws and policies. These 435 people, each representing a specific district, are elected for two-year terms. To be a representative, you must be at least 25 years old, a U.S. citizen for at least seven years, and live in the state you represent. Their job is important for our democracy. They create bills and resolutions, suggest changes, and work on committees. Each representative speaks for their community at the national level, helping to meet the unique needs and concerns of the people they represent. In essence, these representatives are the grassroots link between communities and the federal government. Their job is to make sure the people they represent are heard, their rights are safe, and their needs are taken care of. This local approach is key to having a government that works for its people.

★Success Story Profile: Barbara Lee★

Congresswoman Barbara Lee has been representing California's 12th District (formerly 13th) since 1998. She is the highest-ranking African-American woman in Democratic Leadership, serving as the Co-Chair of the Policy and Steering Committee. She also works on the Budget Committee and the important Appropriations Committee, which looks after all federal government spending.

Barbara Lee's journey, shaped by her experiences with racial barriers and her commitment to justice, began in segregated El Paso,

Texas. Her father was a veteran of two wars and her mother broke many glass ceilings and racial barriers. After grammar school, she moved to California and worked with the local NAACP to integrate her high school cheerleading squad. As a single mother raising two sons, she attended Mills College. As president of the college's Black Student Union, she invited Congresswoman Shirley Chisholm, the first African American woman elected to Congress, to speak on campus. This meeting inspired Lee to register to vote for the first time and work on Chisholm's historic presidential campaign, including serving as her delegate at the 1972 Democratic National Convention.

In 1975, Lee joined Congressman Ron Dellums' staff as an intern and eventually rose to the position of chief of staff. She was one of the few women and people of color in a high-ranking position on Capitol Hill at that time. In 1990, she was elected to the California State Assembly and then to the State Senate in 1996. As a lawmaker, she wrote 67 bills and resolutions that became law. In 1998, Lee was elected to represent California's 9th congressional district (now the 12th) in a special election. She became well-known in 2001 as the only Member of Congress to vote against the authorization for the use of military force (AUMF) after the September 11th events. She believed this would become a blank check for endless war and has been working to repeal it and restore Congress's constitutional oversight on matters of war and peace.

Barbara Lee's political journey is a testament to the courage required to advocate for peace, often standing alone in her convictions. Her solitary vote against the Bush administration's "blank check" to use force post 9/11 was not a momentous decision for her, but a reflection of her moral, ethical, and constitutional beliefs. She draws strength from leaders like Mahatma Gandhi, whose nonviolent resistance liberated India from colonial oppression, and Martin Luther King Jr., who transformed American history through political action. Her philosophy aligns with that of the Dalai Lama, who emphasized that true peace is only possible where human rights are respected, and individuals and nations are free. Despite facing opposition and controversy, Lee remains steadfast in her commitment to justice and peace, embodying the spirit of these influential figures. For twenty-five years, the Barbara Lee Family Foundation has conducted nonpartisan research on women in politics. Their work is guided by our core belief that women's voices strengthen our democracy and enrich our culture.

 Tip

> Research from the Barbara Lee Foundation provides a valuable guide for women running for office based on more than 25 years of research on women's campaigns. These tips can be helpful for all candidates but especially to overcome the obstacles women face with solutions to address them.
>
> 1. **Be prepared**: Lay the groundwork by acquiring and demonstrating the necessary traits and resources. Women candidates often face an "imagination barrier" as voters struggle to picture women in roles historically dominated by white men. The more women candidates run; the more comfortable voters get imagining women holding that seat. Demonstrating qualifications, showing effective leadership, and highlighting expertise all contribute to overcoming this barrier.
>
> 2. **Establish your qualifications:** Be prepared before you publicly announce your plans to run for office. Showcase

your leadership experience and connect your accomplishments to establish your qualifications to be elected, serve, and address the important issues in your community. Create your story or narrative that establishes your qualifications across 360 degrees of your life experience including your professional career, educational, and personal life accomplishments. Also, be sure to contrast your qualifications with those of the opposition. Be honest, stand up for what is right, be knowledgeable, get results, be confident, be organized, have a vision, and stay in touch.

3. **Present to win:** Present your story with messages that resonate, maintain a professional and approachable style, and demonstrate your confidence, qualifications, and competence. Perception is critical to show your readiness to lead. Your presence, which influences perception, includes your appearance, tone of voice, speaking style, and the substance of your communication. Dress appropriately in professional attire for campaign events. Practice delivering a clear, steady, and confident tone of voice. Make and maintain eye contact with your audience to engage and gain their trust. Always be ready to answer hard questions. This shows you know your stuff and helps your audience trust you.

★*Success Story Profile: Knock Down the House*★

"Knock Down the House" is a 2019 documentary film that chronicles the journey of four progressive women who ran for Congress in the 2018 United States elections. The film showcases their grassroots campaigns endorsed by Justice Democrats and Brand New Congress against long-standing incumbents. Alexandria Ocasio-Cortez won her primary and then the general election. This started a trend of progressive women candidates that has kept growing. This led to the creation of the "Squad", a diverse group of progressive Democratic members of the U.S. House of Representatives. They were elected by grassroots organizations and include Alexandria Ocasio-Cortez of New York, Ilhan Omar of Minnesota, Ayanna Pressley of Massachusetts, Rashida Tlaib of Michigan, Jamaal Bowman of New York, Cori Bush of Missouri, Greg Casar of Texas, Summer Lee of Pennsylvania, and many others in state and local positions. These representatives were elected by grassroots people-powered organizations and continue to champion progressive causes in Congress.

Alexandria Ocasio-Cortez, also known as AOC, shows the power of local politics. Born in The Bronx, her path to Congress was influenced by her experiences with racial and economic differences. After the 2008 financial crisis and her father's sudden death, Alexandria worked as a waitress and bartender to help her family. This made her more dedicated to issues affecting working-class people. She became politically active during the 2016 presidential election when she volunteered for Bernie Sanders.

Moved by protests led by indigenous communities at Standing Rock, South Dakota, Alexandria chose to devote her life to serving the public. Just a few months later, she started her first campaign for Congress. Despite being seen as a long shot, her campaign shocked the political establishment when she defeated incumbent Joe Crowley in June 2018. Her campaign was driven entirely by grassroots volunteers and donations, refusing any contributions from corporations.

In January 2019, Alexandria was sworn in as the youngest woman and youngest Latina ever to serve in Congress. As a democratic socialist, she champions progressive policies like a Green New

Deal, envisioning a 10-year national mobilization that would put millions to work in good-paying, union jobs repairing the nation's infrastructure and fighting the intertwined economic, social, racial, and climate crises crippling the country. In her first term, she saw three amendments pass into law, despite Republican control of the Senate and Presidency. She also gained a reputation as an effective questioner in committee hearings, pressuring a major pharmaceutical company into lowering the price of a drug that reduces HIV transmission and forcing a defense contractor to return $16.1 million in federal funding. She also committed to a town hall nearly every month of her first term, hosting a total of 25 town halls.

In January 2021, AOC was sworn in for her second term in Congress. Just a few days later, on January 6, the Capitol was invaded for the first time since the War of 1812. After the attacks, she asked for Members of Congress who had voted against the elections and encouraged the domestic terrorists who attacked the Capitol to be removed. She also voted to impeach President Trump for a second time. Her compelling storytelling skills and activist-legislator approach have made her a political phenomenon, resonating with a new generation of Democrats and challenging established norms.

★Success Story Profile: Maxwell Frost★

Maxwell Alejandro Frost, the first member of Generation Z to be elected to Congress, represents Central Florida in the United States House of Representatives. Frost's journey is as diverse as it is inspiring and brings a fresh, progressive perspective to an institution formerly out of reach for young, working Black and Latino Americans. Adopted at birth and raised in the community he now represents, Frost's advocacy for education was inspired by his mother, a Cuban-American special needs teacher. His father, a full-time musician, ignited his passion for the arts.

Frost's journey into politics began at 15 years old after the tragic mass shooting at Sandy Hook Elementary. He dedicated his life to fighting against gun violence and empowering communities across Florida and the U.S. to get behind gun reform. After surviving a shooting in downtown Orlando in 2016, Frost further committed to fighting for commonsense solutions to this senseless loss of life through leadership roles at the ACLU and March for Our Lives.

He was endorsed by well-known people like Jesse Jackson, former NAACP President Ben Jealous, civil rights activist Dolores Huerta, and U.S. Senators Bernie Sanders and Elizabeth Warren. Frost represents a new generation of political leaders committed to effecting change. Now serving on the Committee on Oversight and Accountability and the Committee on Science, Space, and Technology, Frost is committed to delivering justice and transparency to Floridians while supporting Central Florida's burgeoning status as a simulation tech hub.

Balance Commitments and Responsibilities

Running for office can be a full-time job. You'll need to balance this commitment with your existing responsibilities and understand what serving in the position entails. Before you start your race to victory, it's crucial to thoroughly understand the requirements for the office you are seeking and assess your readiness. To get ready, you need to explore the following questions.

- **Learn about the office:** Identify the office you are interested in and the requirements and qualifications. Reflect on why you are qualified to serve in this role and list three specific reasons. Understand whether it's a partisan or non-partisan office, the length of the term, and any requirements to run for this office.

- **Check-in with those closest to you:** Discuss your potential campaign with your spouse, partner, or closest friends. Consider how a campaign might affect your employment or other obligations.
- **Time commitment:** Evaluate whether running for this position will require a leave of absence from your job or if it will be manageable with your current work and life balance and schedule. Understand the time commitment involved in both campaigning and serving in the position.
- **Finances:** Decide whether you are willing to spend personal finances on this race and how much you are willing to spend. Understand what previous candidates for this office have spent or raised, and whether you are willing to ask others to donate to your campaign. Ensure you are current with your local, state, and federal taxes and have no outstanding debts owed to the government.

 Tip

Before you commit to running for office, you need to understand what it entails and whether you're ready for the challenge. It is not an overnight decision. It is important to take some time to explore your readiness, resources, and commitment. Reflect and review your self-assessment across your diverse experiences in your personal, professional, community, and public service life. Be open and thoughtful about your strengths and weaknesses and level of experience, expertise, and community involvement. This will help you prepare your fit for your political campaign.

1. **Explore your community connections:** Think about your relationship with the community where you plan to run for office. How long have you lived there? Does your family have a history in the community?

2. **Apply your relevant experience:** What is your current occupation and job experience? Is it relevant to the position? Are you a member of professional organizations and groups? What areas of visible accomplishments have you demonstrated in the community? Published works, awards, and public recognition?

3. **Evaluate leadership experience:** Evaluate your participation in community organizations and volunteer activities. Have you held leadership roles in the community? Do you serve or make charitable contributions to organizations and causes relevant to the elected office?

4. **Vote and serve on community boards:** Have you participated in boards, commissions, or non-profit boards? Do you have elected office experience? Have you run for office in the past or been nominated to a non-elected position or committee? What is your fundraising and organizing experience? What is your voting history?

5. **Apply relevant skills and experience:** Assess your skills such as public speaking, debate, fundraising, media experience, policy analysis, and advocacy.

6. **Extracurricular involvement:** Do you participate in

> local clubs, sports, or community events as an artist, musician, parent, or student?

Explore Your Opportunity

The exploratory phase is a crucial step in your journey to run for office. This involves understanding the requirements of the office you're aiming for, evaluating your core network's support, and considering potential conflicts with your employment or other responsibilities. Familiarize yourself with finance laws and reporting requirements for political offices in your district.

Analyze the top three issues your campaign will focus on. Understand the prevailing solutions and plans for these issues and consider how your unique skills or specialized experience can contribute to these solutions.

Do a self-assessment and think about what you are good at and what you could improve. This will help you get ready for the campaign and let you put together a team that works well with your skills and personality.

Make sure you know the specific requirements and timing needed to file your candidacy for office before you're ready to announce. Explore the issues that will be relevant for this election in your community and develop your story and positioning statements.

Evaluate Your Strengths and Weaknesses

Getting ready for a political campaign means thinking about what you are good at and what you could improve. You should also get feedback from close friends, family, and people in your local community to get a full picture of your qualities. Here are some things to think about:

- **Compassion:** Are you good at understanding other people's feelings and caring about their needs?
- **Confidence:** Do you exude confidence in your abilities and ideas?
- **Honesty and integrity**: Are you perceived as trustworthy and transparent?
- **Listening skills:** Are you a good listener? Do you make others feel heard and understood?
- **Name recognition:** Remembering names can be a valuable skill in politics where building personal connections is important.
- **Public speaking and storytelling:** Are you comfortable speaking in front of large groups?
- **Sense of humor:** A good sense of humor can make people feel more connected to you.
- **Writing skills:** Can you write in a way that gets your point across?

Self-reflection can help you understand how others see you, which is important in politics where how people see you is everything. Reflecting on these areas can help identify where you excel and where there might be room for improvement. It can also guide the formation of your core team by highlighting the characteristics needed to complement your own. Spend some time thinking about these questions:

- What are the things you are good at?
- What is the one thing you could get better at?

- Describe yourself in three words.
- What charity or community area is most important to you?
- Do you have the necessary life experience?
- Would you vote for yourself?

 **Tip**

> It can be beneficial to seek feedback from friends, family, and colleagues as well. Their perspectives can provide valuable insights into how others perceive you. Ask people you trust in your community, like your family, friends, and supporters, to fill out a survey to give you feedback.
>
> 1. **Public speaking skills**: How would you rate my public speaking skills on a scale of 1-10?
>
> 2. **Leadership skills**: Can you provide examples of when I demonstrated strong leadership skills?
>
> 3. **Community involvement**: How involved do you think I am in the community?
>
> 4. **Voter confidence:** If I run for office, would you vote for me? Why or why not?
>
> 5. **Feedback:** Please share any other comments or feedback. Your thoughts are important and can help me understand how others see me.

Explore the Needs in Your Community

Next, continue your exploration phase and take the necessary time to dive deeper and learn about the needs of your district. What are the important issues and needs at this time for you to understand in depth during your candidacy and to represent your constituents when elected to office? What are the cultural, community, and economic factors that impact the lives of the people that you will need to engage with to be successful in your campaign? Are you able to engage these people with enthusiasm, energy, and electability and have the drive and determination to represent them all and the important issues aligned with your values and goals?

- **Demographics**: Understand the ethnic, educational, and economic breakdown of your district. Analyze voting patterns and trends.
- **Community influencers**: Identify the most influential people in your district. Engage with local thought leaders, heads of non-profits, labor leaders, party committee chairs, business leaders, and media figures.
- **District characteristics**: Understand what distinguishes your district. Who are the major employers? What cultural institutions, sports teams, or educational institutions are there? What industries are unique to your district?
- **Elected official history**: Learn about current and past elected officials. Seek advice from them and understand the history of the office you're running for.
- **Key issues**: Identify the hot-button issues in your district. Understand the organizations and leaders on each side of these issues.
- **Party endorsements**: Understand how to secure your party's endorsement. Engage with active party clubs in your area.

- **Fundraising**: Plan your fundraising strategy. Who will be your initial donors?

By exploring these areas, you will gain a better understanding of your district and be better prepared to represent its needs.

Engage with Political Training Organizations

There are many groups and resources available to help you get ready to run for office.

- **Arena:** Arena Academy was created to help the many people who got into politics after Donald Trump was elected. The organization provides training programs for aspiring campaign staff, connects Academy graduates with career opportunities, and offers a collection of free toolkits, tutorials, and templates for building winning campaigns.
- **Candidate Boot Camp:** Candidate Boot Camp is a team of experienced campaign professionals that offers online candidate training and free resources. The training is non-partisan and works to make democracy more accessible by making it easier to run for political office.
- **Close the Gap California:** Close the Gap California is a campaign that works all over the state. Its goal is to close the gender gap in the California Legislature by 2028. They recruit accomplished, progressive women in targeted districts and prepare them to launch competitive campaigns.
- **Democratic Party Training Resources:** As the largest Democratic campaign training organization in the nation, they provide Democratic candidates, campaign staffers, and

- **Emerge:** Emerge is a nationally recognized organization that recruits and trains Democratic women to run for office. Emerge has trained over 5,000 people and oversees locally-based training programs. They aim to reach 100% gender parity in elected offices nationwide.
- **Run for Something:** Launched in 2017, Run for Something recruits and supports young, diverse progressives to run for down-ballot races to build sustainable power for Democrats in all 50 states. The organization lowers the barriers to entry for these candidates by providing tactical and strategic support, advice, mentorship, access to training, and more.
- **Vote, Run, Lead:** Vote Run Lead is a team of dreamers, activists, strategists, and movement leaders dedicated to advancing women's representation across all levels of government. Their alumni serve on city councils, county boards, state houses, supreme courts, and Congress.

Set Up Your Candidate Campaign Team

Before you announce that you're running for office, it's important to put together your campaign team and plan how you'll announce it. Here are some steps to get you started:

- **Build your team:** Start with friends, family, neighbors, and community leaders. Consider forming a steering committee for advice and networking. Your fundraising committee can be invaluable, especially if it includes someone experienced in fundraising or money management.
- **Define priority roles:** Key roles in a political campaign

include the candidate, campaign manager, fundraising director, communications director, networking director, and events director. Depending on the size of your campaign, you might fill several of these roles yourself or delegate them to volunteers or paid professionals if you have a budget.

- **Leverage volunteer strengths**: Every volunteer brings unique strengths to the table. Find tasks that align with their skills and personality, even if they aren't comfortable with public-facing roles.

- **Plan your announcement:** Review your plan calendar backward from the day of the election and map your goals and strategy with a timeline and key events and milestones to win the election.

- **Understand the endorsement process:** Endorsements can significantly boost your campaign, so understanding the endorsement process is key. Craft your campaign message for print, online, and speaking events such as debates, forums, town halls, and endorsement meetings.

Running a grassroots campaign often means operating with limited resources. Building a strong volunteer team can be a game-changer in such scenarios.

Prepare for Your Announcement

Before announcing your candidacy, it is crucial to craft a clear, concise, and consistent message and story. Words do matter. Your message should be genuine, address key issues, and reflect your values and experiences. It should set you apart from other candidates and connect with voters in your community, including families, students, businesses, unions, and other key groups.

Your campaign story should be simple and easy to grasp. It should win the "*hearts*" and "*minds*" of voters with messages and images that support your narrative about why you are the best candidate for the job. It should convey that you understand and support the community's needs and values and that you're prepared to deliver on your promises as an elected leader. Words matter - what you say in speeches, debates, on your website, social media, signs, and door hangers needs to reflect your commitment to serving your community.

Develop a 60-second "elevator" speech on why you should be the next office holder and what you will do for people. This is your first and best chance to leave a good impression on a potential supporter. Be considerate, take your time, and be true to yourself.

- What is your message?
- Why are you running?
- What do you want to accomplish with your announcement?
- What is the look/feel you're going for?
- Should this be an event?

Before announcing your candidacy, it is crucial to strategize and set goals for your campaign.

- **Set goals**: Estimate the number of votes you will need to win the election. Review results from previous elections for voter turnout and margin of victory. Understand factors like voter turnout during a Presidential election, running against an incumbent, and the impact of a primary.
- **Budget**: Evaluate your budget and determine the total amount

needed to win the election, as well as the timing and schedule of budget allocation during the election phases. Many candidates lose elections due to not being able to deliver on the plan and budget at the right time.

- **Announce**: Plan your announcement carefully. Consider hosting an event where you can invite supporters and media and share it online via a webcast and social media. Having supporters and endorsing influencers speak at the event can be impactful. Build momentum online and through your email campaign list.
- **Deliver your message**: Prepare and practice your story so that you are comfortable and consistent. You'll have many opportunities to deliver your message during your campaign, from your first announcement to endorsement meetings, debates, town hall forums, campaign events, and speaking directly with voters.

Keep your message simple, memorable, and focused. Start with a clear opening, explain who you are and why you're running, share your ideas, and close with an ask for their vote, donation, and volunteer support.

Budget for Your Campaign

Determining your campaign budget can be challenging, especially for first-time candidates. One approach is to review campaign disclosures from previous campaigns to get an estimate of potential costs. Prioritize spending on items that will help you earn more votes. Not all campaigns will require every item on this list.

Your campaign budget should include operational costs such as salaries, voter files and databases, website, gas, office space, bank and payment processing fees, and office supplies. Voter contact expenses might include direct mail, radio ads, digital advertising, live & automated calls, palm cards, business cards, yard signs, banners, and newspaper ads.

Don't forget to budget for volunteer expenses related to canvassing, community meetings, and get out the vote, or GOTV operations. Fundraising costs might include fundraising events, printing, postage, letterhead and envelopes, and donation cards. Not all campaigns will require every item on this list. Prioritize based on your campaign's specific needs and resources.

Communications, Data, and Digital Strategy

Effective communication, both external and internal, is crucial for a successful campaign.

- **Data-driven approach:** Utilize voter files and digital information to build your internal and external contacts. This data can provide valuable insights into your audience's preferences and behaviors, allowing you to tailor your communications accordingly. Data should inform all aspects of your campaign, from your messaging to your outreach efforts.
- **Internal communications**: Keeping your team informed and consistent with the campaign message is vital. Regular communication ensures efficient use of volunteers' time and keeps everyone on the same page. Ideally, have a communications director to vet any work done by the team before it goes public. Collaboration with instant messages, Slack, and other digital communications tools for rapid response and collaboration.
- **External communications**: This involves delivering your message to the outside world. Consider paid media options

such as newspaper, print, digital, radio, and television ads. Earned media, like news stories or community access cable shows, can also be valuable. Social media is a must for any political candidate - start with creating a public Facebook page and ensure your LinkedIn profile is up to date. Video and digital images should be prioritized including videos for TikTok, YouTube, Facebook, Instagram, and other social media channels.

 **Tip**

Here are some ideas for using digital strategies for external communications:

1. **Send email:** Use email contacts to build a loyal and engaged subscriber base and send personalized and relevant messages based on voter data and segmentation.

2. **Build a website:** Make a website that shares your vision, values, and policies, and tells people how to donate, volunteer, and vote.

3. **Amplify with social media:** Use social media to reach and talk with a wide and diverse audience, and share interesting stories, testimonials, and endorsements.

4. **Share videos:** Make and share high-quality videos on platforms like TikTok, YouTube, Facebook, and Instagram. You can use these videos to show off your personality, achievements, and campaign events.

> 5. **Optimize for mobile devices:** Optimize your digital content and design for mobile devices, especially for younger voters who are more likely to access information and participate in online activities through their smartphones.

In the digital age, a successful campaign strategy should integrate both in-person and online communications for broader reach and impact. Establish your online presence across platforms like social media, email newsletters, and your campaign website, and keep them updated with engaging content. This integrated approach, rather than a siloed one, will create a more cohesive and effective campaign.

Chapter Checklist: Run for Office

Congratulations! You have taken significant strides toward launching your campaign for office. You've explored various opportunities, conducted a thorough self-assessment, and engaged with your core network of supporters. Running for office is not just about winning an election; it is about making a difference in your community.

Inspired by historic progressive leaders like Shirley Chisholm and Barbara Lee, as well as current trailblazers like the Squad you are now ready to take the next step. In the next chapter, you will create your message, platform, and communication process to get ready to go with your campaign launch.

Checklist: In this chapter, you learned how to run for office. Running for office is an opportunity to dive into democracy. You explored various elected and nominated positions in your desired district, assessed your readiness and fit, and prepared the resources, support, and strategy needed to win your race. Here are some key takeaways from this chapter:

1. You matched your passion and purpose with the right opportunities and made sure you were the right person for the job.

2. Being a candidate can feel like a full-time job. You balanced this commitment with your existing responsibilities and understood what serving in the position entails.

3. You familiarized yourself with the rules, timelines, and schedules specific to the office you were running for. You navigated your political journey according to the type of election and race.

4. You assembled a team to investigate fundraising and voter outreach strategies before filing your candidacy. You planned your public announcement, built your volunteer base, started your fundraising campaign, and identified target voter strategies.

5. You found the office you wanted to run for, assessed your fit, assembled your campaign committee, and prepared to launch your campaign. You put your name on the ballot and took your first steps toward victory.

Six

Craft Your Message

I have a dream that my four little children will one day live in a nation where they will not be judged by the color of their skin but by the content of their character.

–Martin Luther King, Jr.

Martin Luther King Jr was a minister, activist, political philosopher, a pre-eminent advocate of nonviolence, and one of the most important leaders in the civil rights movement.

Born in Atlanta, Georgia, King followed his father and grandfather into the ministry, eventually earning a doctorate from Boston University. Inspired by his Christian faith, the teachings of Mahatma Gandhi, and the influence of Howard Thurman, King led a nonviolent movement in the late 1950s and 1960s to achieve legal equality for African Americans in the United States. Professor Thurman at Boston University introduced King to the concept of nonviolence and civil disobedience.

King used these principles to lead a movement in the late 1950s and '60s that aimed to give African Americans equal rights under the law. He served on the NAACP's executive committee and led the Montgomery Bus Boycott in 1955. This peaceful protest against racial segregation on public buses lasted over a year and ended with a Supreme Court ruling that made segregation on buses illegal.

Dr. King's influence extended beyond this landmark event. He traveled extensively, delivering powerful speeches and leading peaceful protests. In 1963, Martin Luther King, Jr, and various civil rights groups rallied over 250,000 people in Washington D.C. to advocate for the rights of Black Americans. His *"I Have a Dream"* speech on the Lincoln Memorial steps amplified the Civil Rights Movement's message to a broader audience. Despite facing arrests and threats, King's commitment to nonviolent resistance won him the Nobel Peace Prize at 35. His life ended abruptly when he was assassinated in 1968, but his legacy continues to inspire equality and justice movements worldwide.

This chapter is about turning your dream into reality. It guides you to craft your key messages, build a platform that caters to your community's needs, and effectively communicate your message through various channels and events. You will learn to define a clear, concise, and compelling message and story.

- **Define a clear and compelling message and story:** Your message should be clear, concise, and compelling. It should resonate with your target audience's values and interests. It is the story to articulate the vision, mission, and goals of the campaign, candidacy, or cause.
- **Develop your platform:** You will develop your platform, processes, and digital strategy to deliver relevant and impactful messages to reach the targeted audiences in your community. Your platform will bring light to the most important issues impacting your community.
- **Communicate your message effectively:** Explore best

practices and tips to communicate your message effectively through various channels and events both in-person, online, and in virtual hybrid formats.

Target Your Audience

In the preceding chapters, you engaged with your community to research their needs, values, and interests. Your goal is to understand your audience's interests, desires, and fears. You can further research demographic data, voter records, surveys, polls, focus groups, interviews, and social media if necessary.

Segmenting your audience helps you to create tailored messages that resonate deeply with specific groups, leading to more engagement and support. By understanding your community's needs, priorities, and concerns, your messages and stories become more authentic and empathetic. This section will guide you in defining a clear, concise, and compelling message that aligns with your target audience's values and interests. Here are some factors to consider when segmenting your audience:

- **Demographics:** Think about age, gender, income level, education level, marital status, and occupation.
- **Interests and issues**: Determine the key issues and interests that appeal to your audience. These could range from climate change and healthcare to education and civil rights.
- **Location:** Geographic location can play a significant role in shaping people's experiences and perspectives. Consider segmenting your audience based on urban vs. rural areas, regions, or specific communities.
- **Race and ethnicity:** Different racial and ethnic groups may

have unique experiences and concerns that should be acknowledged and addressed in your campaign messaging.
- **Political party or philosophy:** People's political affiliations or philosophies can significantly influence their views on various issues. Understanding these can help tailor your message to resonate with different political groups.
- **Voting records:** Past voting behavior can be a strong indicator of future actions. Consider segmenting your audience based on their voting history.

The goal of audience segmentation is to understand the diverse needs and interests of your audience so you can create a message that resonates with each distinct group. By employing effective segmentation, targeting, and positioning, your message and narrative will not only reach the right ears but will also strike a chord, reflecting the values, interests, and needs of each audience. This tailored approach amplifies the power and impact of your message, making it a powerful tool in your campaign, candidacy, or cause. Here are some examples:

- **Bernie Sanders' 2016 Presidential Campaign:** Sanders targeted rural America, focusing on the first two primary audiences in Iowa and New Hampshire with an inspirational video featuring Simon and Garfunkel's 1968 song *"America"*. The video showcased images of packed campaign rallies and meet-and-greet events, interspersed with scenes of American flags and the Iowa skyline. The song's lyrics *"They've all come to look for America..."* echoed the campaign's message of unity and hope.
- **March for Our Lives**: Started by Parkland high school shooting survivors, this student-led group advocates for gun

control and stricter regulations to prevent gun violence in the U.S. Their 2018 rally in Washington D.C. attracted over 200,000 people, with around 800 similar marches held nationwide. Their message was clear, *"We, as youth, must now be the change that we seek. If you don't stand for something, you'll fall for anything."*

- **Sunrise Movement:** This group targets a younger generation of activists who will be most affected by the impacts of climate change. By understanding their audience's concerns and aspirations, they can focus on crafting messages that deeply resonate and spur action. Their call to action is clear and compelling: *"To stop climate change, we need to change everything. Therefore, we have to take over."*

Create Your Message

Now, it is time to create your message and story for the target audiences for your campaign, candidacy, or cause. Create a clear message that aligns with your community's values and concerns. This involves sharing stories about real people and providing specific examples, using vivid language that inspires mental images, and helping each individual feel a personal connection. This approach ensures that your message is not only heard but also felt, leading to a deeper level of engagement and support.

Your vision, mission, and goals can be summarized in a clear and concise message. This message should tell a compelling narrative that connects with your audience's problems and aspirations. It should highlight the benefits and advantages of supporting your cause, contrasting them with the alternatives. Most importantly, it should include a strong call to action that motivates your audience to support your cause.

Your message acts as a bridge between your campaign, candidate, or cause and your audience. It provides the who, why, and what to compel action. Who represents your campaign, candidate, or cause, and the target audience you need to reach? Why is the compelling need, issue, or reason behind the cause that inspires interest and engagement? How is the solution that addresses the problem and the call to action to make an impact? Your messages should be clear and concise. Start with simple bullet points, then expand these into short elevator pitches of 30, 60, and 90 words. Then develop these into detailed position statements for use on your website and in endorsements.

Develop Your Personal Story

Your personal story is a powerful tool as an organizer, candidate, or activist. It's not just about your stance on an issue or candidate, but how your life experiences have shaped your perspectives and values. Consider these questions when developing your story:

- What motivates you to act and could potentially inspire others?
- Can you share personal stories about specific people or events that demonstrate how you've learned or acted on these values?
- What action will you ask others to take? Share the petition? Submit feedback? Act?

Now, it's time to craft your message and narrative for the target audiences of your campaign, candidacy, or cause. Let's consider a few examples:

- Perhaps you are a schoolteacher in a low-income area, where many of your students face significant disadvantages. Discuss how this situation impacts your teaching effectiveness and the extra efforts you make to ensure student success. This personal experience could tie into broader issues like income inequality and the need for a living wage.

- Or maybe you are a recent college graduate struggling with student debt, having trouble finding work that pays well enough to allow you to pay down these loans. This personal experience could tie into broader issues like the need for more affordable or free public college education.

- Alternatively, you could be someone nearing retirement, working part-time, and volunteering in the community to address food poverty issues. Share your experiences and the challenges you face when recruiting support for your cause. Your narrative could highlight the need for community engagement, donations, and volunteers to combat food poverty.

These success story profiles underscore the importance of crafting a clear, concise, and compelling message that resonates with your target audience's values and interests. Before finalizing your message, research, test, and share your draft message with supporters for feedback. Words matter, and reviewing with another person for feedback will improve your story and ensure your message is clear and relevant. This tailored approach amplifies the power and impact of your message, making it a powerful tool in your campaign, candidacy, or cause.

★Success Story Profile: Fridays for Future★

Fridays for Future (FFF) is a global climate strike movement that began in August 2018. The movement was initiated by 15-year-old Greta Thunberg, who started a school strike for climate action. Frustrated by society's lack of urgency towards the climate crisis, she sat outside the Swedish Parliament every school day for three weeks leading up to the Swedish election, demanding immediate action.

Initially, Greta was alone in her protest. However, she was soon joined by others. On September 8th, Greta and her fellow school strikers decided to continue their strike until Swedish policies aligned with the Paris Agreement. They created the hashtag #FridaysForFuture and encouraged young people worldwide to join them. This marked the beginning of the global school strike for climate.

- **School #ClimateStrike - All You Need to Know:** Students are walking out of school and going on #ClimateStrike to call on governments to keep warming below the unacceptably dangerous level of 1.5 degrees Celsius and protect our future.

- **Why We Strike:** Climate change is already a deadly reality with heat waves, floods, and hurricanes killing hundreds and devastating communities across the world. Despite the latest stark warning from climate scientists that we have only 12 years to reverse course, politicians are ignoring their call.

- **When We Strike:** Every Friday is a #ClimateStrike day.

- **Where We Strike:** Your school, a government office - anywhere you feel called to make a stand.

- **More Information:** We have resources available for students, parents, teachers, and school staff. Join us in making a difference!

This message targets specific audiences, students, parents, teachers, and staff, with a clear what, why, when, where, and call to action that ignited an international awakening. Students and activists worldwide began protesting outside their local parliaments and city halls. Fridays for Future, along with other groups across the world, represents a hopeful new wave of change. They have inspired millions of people to act on the climate crisis. They localized the content with translations available in several languages including French, German, Polish, Spanish, Portuguese, Italian, Chinese, Russian, Slovak, Finnish, Albanian, Serbian, Arabic, and Ukrainian.

★*Success Story Profile: Mexipets Animal Rescue*★

Mexipets Animal Rescue is a nonprofit that works to enhance the well-being of cats and dogs in rural Mexico, a region plagued by overpopulation, abuse, and neglect. The organization raises funds for spay and neuter campaigns and encourages the adoption of Mexican street animals in the U.S. through the Paws Without Borders flights.

Mexipets Animal Rescue serves as an excellent example of a clear, targeted, and compelling message that effectively addresses the needs of its audience. This nonprofit organization, dedicated to improving the lives of cats and dogs in rural Mexico, has successfully harnessed the power of storytelling and targeted messaging to engage its audience and inspire action.

Their focus is clear: addressing the overpopulation, abuse, and neglect of animals in rural Mexico through spay and neuter campaigns and promoting the adoption of Mexican street animals in the U.S. By targeting animal lovers and potential volunteers in the U.S., they have created a bridge between the needs of animals in Mexico and those who can provide help.

Mexipets engages its community with heartwarming images of adopted cats, dogs, and their happy owners. This approach not only raises awareness about the plight of animals in rural Mexico but also encourages more people to support their cause through donations, volunteering, or adoption.

The organization's promotional activities, which rely on word-of-mouth referrals and social media outreach through Facebook, are tailored to their audience's preferences and behaviors. Their vibrant branding, reflected in their t-shirts, mirrors the spirit of Mexico and its cats and dogs, creating a visual connection with their cause.

Repeat Your Message to Build Your Brand

Consistency is important when delivering your message across various venues and engagement channels, ranging from in-person conversations to digital platforms, social media, and traditional media. As you share your message and story, you are simultaneously building your brand. Being consistent with words and images across all channels not only reinforces your message but also cultivates a strong, recognizable brand for your campaign, candidate, or cause.

Keep your message simple, authentic, and consistent, and do not hesitate to repeat it frequently. Given that people's attention spans are generally short, a simple, consistent message stands a better chance of being heard and remembered. Repetition of your message is crucial to ensure it resonates with your audience. Be consistent across multiple communication channels to amplify your message. This can include your emails, social media posts, phone banking, flyers in local venues, and more. Be sure that your narrative, visual elements like photos and videos, and communication channels consistently reflect the values and mission of your campaign. Keep sharing your message and engaging with your audience, and over time, you will see your impact grow.

 Tip

> Creating digital assets that align with your message and brand is a crucial step in promoting your message. Your digital assets are an extension of your campaign, candidate, or cause. They should not only look professional but also convey your message and inspire action. These assets will be used across various platforms, both online and offline. Here are some tips:
>
> 1. **Be consistent:** Make sure your digital assets align with your brand identity and voice, including colors, fonts, logos, and other visual elements that represent your brand.
>
> 2. **Support unions:** Work with a union to create your digital assets. This not only supports fair labor practices but also ensures high-quality production. Be sure to include the union label on all assets to show your support for union labor.
>
> 3. **Understand requirements:** Your political candidate messaging will need to be persuasive and consistent for potential voters and supporters to convey a clear and compelling vision, values, and policies of the candidate, and to inspire and mobilize people to act. The message should be memorable, distinctive, and relevant to the office and the district to showcase the candidate's biography, platform, endorsements, events, and contact information and comply

with the legal requirements of the jurisdiction, such as contribution limits, disclosure rules, and funding sources.

4. **Design for mobile and multiple platforms:** Design your assets for use across various platforms. This includes your website, email campaigns, social media platforms, as well as in-person materials like yard signs and banners.

5. **Be clear:** Ensure that your message is clear and easily understood in all assets. Avoid cluttering designs with too much text or complex visuals.

6. **Include a call to action:** Include a clear call to action in your assets. Whether it's asking viewers to donate, volunteer, or vote, make sure it's easy for them to understand what you want them to do.

7. **Test and refine:** Test your assets across different platforms to see how they look and perform. Use this feedback to refine your designs and improve their effectiveness.

Develop Your Platform

In your journey to becoming a change agent in your community with a clear crafted message, the next step is to develop your platform. Your platform provides the foundation for your message, your processes, and your digital strategy, helping you to deliver relevant and impactful messages that reach the targeted audiences in your community. It is not just about broadcasting your message; it is about creating structures and processes to be consistent and reach your targeted audiences with consistent messages and build awareness for your brand.

Your platform and content calendar connect your message with your audience, share your vision, and rally support for your cause. It will reflect the values and interests of your community, ensuring that your message resonates with those you aim to serve. In the following section, we will delve into the specifics of how to build this platform effectively, keeping in mind the importance of authenticity, consistency, and engagement.

Plan Your Content Calendar

As you transition from crafting a consistent message for sharing across various audiences and mediums, it is helpful to create a content calendar. This tool is very useful for navigating the complexity of messages, audiences, and versions of your content and to help plan your content distribution. It is essential to have a structured approach. Whether you are using a whiteboard, a computer program, or a simple piece of paper, laying out your calendar is crucial. It provides a clear roadmap for your content creation process and message delivery process when to launch campaigns, host events, and allocate resources.

- **Structure:** Define the different types of activities for your campaign. This could range from volunteer recruiting and training to creating your message and content, securing endorsements, organizing rallies, and scheduling debates.
- **Timing:** Understand the schedule and duration of your campaign. It could be as short as a single weekend event or as long as a two-year roadmap.
- **Categories:** Come up with categories for the types of

activities you'll need to add to your calendar such as volunteer recruiting and training, creating your message and content, endorsements, rallies, and debates.

- **Digital tools**: Update the calendar digitally to ensure you are still on target in terms of the types of events, meetings, and expected outcomes.
- **Event planning:** Consider potential conflicts with holidays or other special events like major sporting events. Plan around these to take advantage of increased awareness.
- **Communication channels:** Use multiple channels of communication to get people to show up at your events. This could include email, social media, phone banking, and flyers in local venues.
- **Goals and objectives:** Map your goals and objectives based on the phases of your campaign. This will help you stay focused and ensure you're making progress towards your goals.

 Tip

> Pictures are worth a thousand words. Be sure to capture photos and creative visual images to support your message and content strategy. Visual imagery can create personal connections and trust in political campaigns. Here's how to use images and visuals effectively:
>
> 1. **Capture images at events:** Take captivating photos at events like door-knocking, rallies, and debates. These images can create a personal connection and build trust with the audience.

2. **Create images for print and digital assets:** Use high-quality images of the candidate on yard signs, postcards, and other print materials. These visuals not only catch the eye but also help voters recognize and remember the candidate.

3. **Share videos:** Videos are a powerful tool for sharing the candidate's story and message. Live streaming events and making them available on-demand can help reach a wider audience.

4. **Capture supporter stories:** Capture compelling stories from supporters, volunteers, and endorsers of the campaign. These testimonials can be powerful tools for building trust and showing the impact of the campaign on real people.

5. **Maintain a content calendar:** Plan your content calendar strategically to ensure you have a steady stream of fresh, engaging images to share. This includes planning for specific events, holidays, or key dates in the campaign.

Communicate Your Message Effectively

Consistently sharing your story, both in person and through digital tools, is crucial for effective message dissemination. Authenticity and repetition are key elements in this process. By continually engaging with your audience and sharing your message, you'll see your impact grow over time.

Crafting your message effectively is crucial for your campaign, candidate, or cause. Explore these best practices and tips to communicate your message through various channels and events, both in-person and online.

In-person communication is the most powerful. Public speaking at events, community meetings, or rallies allows you to share your story and connect with people on a personal level. Networking at relevant events can help spread your message through word of mouth, reaching individuals who may not be accessible through digital.

Engaging with digital platforms is equally important. Sharing your story on social media platforms like Facebook, Instagram, LinkedIn, TikTok, and YouTube, using appropriate hashtags, can increase visibility and encourage viral sharing. Email newsletters, listservs, and forums can be particularly effective for reaching a targeted audience. Posting your story on relevant websites and blogs can help reach a wider audience and establish credibility. Setting up Google Alerts can help track your online impact by notifying you when your campaign, candidate, or cause is mentioned online.

Earning media attention can further amplify your message. Consider expanding your story to other publications or writing additional articles on related topics. If you enjoy writing, joining a local writers' club or union can provide opportunities for learning, networking, and potentially gaining press credentials to submit stories and articles. These strategies demonstrate the power of organized, community-driven action in effecting meaningful change.

Success Story Profiles

Take a few minutes to review these success story profiles that showcase best practices to effectively define clear, compelling messages and stories that resonate with their target audience's values and interests. They developed robust platforms and digital strategies to deliver relevant and impactful messages, shedding light on the most important issues impacting their communities. These success stories also highlight effective communication practices, demonstrating how to convey messages effectively through various channels and events, both in-person and online. They offer valuable insights and lessons on how to craft and deliver a powerful message for maximum impact.

★Success Story Profile: Robert Reich★

Robert Bernard Reich, a renowned professor, author, lawyer, and political commentator, has made significant contributions to various administrations, including those of Presidents Gerald Ford, Jimmy Carter, and Bill Clinton.

He has authored eighteen books, co-created two influential films, and designed a course at UC Berkeley titled "Wealth and Poverty". His work has shaped many students' perspectives on wealth disparity and economic policy, inspiring a new generation of leaders to strive for a more equitable future.

His 2013 documentary, "Inequality for All", based on his book "Aftershock: The Next Economy and America's Future", explores the widening income inequality in the United States. The film is a powerful exploration of the causes and consequences of wealth imbalance in the United States and its impact on democracy.

- **Consistent message:** Reich's consistent focus on income inequality and economic policy across his books, films, and courses demonstrates the power of consistent messaging and has reinforced his message and built a strong, recognizable brand.
- **Multiple platforms:** He has effectively published across multiple platforms - from traditional books and in-person teaching to digital mediums including documentaries and social media- to reach a wide audience and amplify his message.

★ Success Story: Alexandria Ocasio-Cortez ★

Alexandria Ocasio-Cortez's campaign is a prime example of how effective messaging and branding can significantly impact a political campaign. She won on the issues working hard to get out the vote in her community and her campaign brand and assets reflected her energy, spirit, and community commitment. Here are some key elements that contributed to her success:

- **Authentic:** The campaign's visual brand was a true reflection of Ocasio-Cortez herself, embodying her revolutionary spirit and progressive ideals. This authenticity resonated with voters and helped build trust.
- **Inclusive messaging:** The campaign's messaging was inclusive, and representative of the diverse community Ocasio-Cortez was serving. The use of bilingual posters and the incorporation of elements from her Puerto Rican heritage helped connect with a broad range of voters.
- **Bold design:** Ocasio-Cortez's campaign used vibrant colors and bold typography to stand out. Her posters, featuring her last name bookended by Spanish exclamation points, were attention-grabbing and communicated her energy and passion.
- **Strategic use of color:** The campaign deviated from the traditional red and blue political branding, incorporating yellow for positivity and purple to represent unity. This strategic use of color helped differentiate her campaign from others.
- **Effective engagement:** Ocasio-Cortez's campaign effectively engaged with the community, focusing on turning out young people and people of color. This grassroots approach, combined with a strong online presence, helped mobilize support and drive voter turnout.

★Success Story Profile: Colin Kaepernick★

Colin Kaepernick, also known as Kap, is a former Super Bowl quarterback who knelt during "The Star-Spangled Banner" in 2016 to highlight systemic oppression, particularly police violence, against Black and Brown individuals.

Despite being denied employment by the league, Kaepernick has since founded and helped fund three organizations—Know Your Rights Camp, Ra Vision Media, and Kaepernick Publishing—that together advance the liberation of Black and Brown people through storytelling, systems change, and political education.

In a unique partnership, Ben & Jerry's teamed up with Kaepernick to launch a new ice cream flavor called "Change the Whirled." This caramel non-dairy frozen dessert was created to celebrate Kaepernick's courageous work to confront systemic oppression and stop police violence against Black and Brown people. Kaepernick's portion of the proceeds from "Change the Whirled" goes to his Know Your Rights campaign, a nonprofit devoted to Black and Brown communities. This partnership shows the power of aligning a brand with a progressive cause.

- **Clear, concise, and consistent:** Kap's act of kneeling during the national anthem shows the power of a clear, concise, and compelling message that resonated with many and brought attention to systemic oppression and police violence.
- **Multiple platforms:** He effectively used multiple platforms as a professional athlete, his partnerships with organizations like Ben & Jerry's, and his organizations to amplify his message and make a significant impact.

★ Success Story Profile: Al Gore ★

Al Gore, the 45th vice president of the United States, is a prominent figure in the fight against climate change. He founded and chairs The Climate Reality Project and has produced award-winning documentaries like "An Inconvenient Truth" and its sequel, "An Inconvenient Sequel: Truth to Power." His efforts in raising awareness about climate change earned him, along with the Intergovernmental Panel on Climate Change, the Nobel Peace Prize in 2007.

Gore's collaboration with Nancy Duarte led to the creation of his impactful presentation, "An Inconvenient Truth," which evolved into a significant data story influencing the climate change movement. Duarte's team transformed raw data into captivating charts and infographics, making the complex issue of climate change more accessible and understandable. As Gore traveled globally, localized content was added to his core presentation, ensuring resonance with diverse audiences. The slides from "An Inconvenient Truth" informed the film of the same name, which raised global awareness about global warming and revitalized the environmental movement.

- **Compelling story**: Gore's campaign on climate change serves as an excellent example of how a clear, consistent, and compelling message can drive a movement.
- **Data Visualization**: The transformation of raw data into captivating charts and infographics made the complex issue of climate change more accessible and understandable to the public.
- **Adaptability**: The supplementation of Gore's core presentation with localized content for regional audiences ensured that the message resonated with diverse audiences globally.
- **Influence and Impact**: The film "An Inconvenient Truth",

informed by the slides from Gore's presentation, raised global awareness about global warming and revitalized the environmental movement. This showcases the power of a well-crafted message in inspiring action on a crucial issue.

Chapter Checklist: Craft Your Message

In this chapter, you have learned how to create your message, develop your platform, and successfully communicate your story for a campaign, candidate, or cause. Here's a summary checklist of the lessons learned:

Checklist:

1. You crafted a clear, concise, and compelling message that resonates with your target audience and articulates the vision, mission, and goals of your campaign, candidacy, or cause.
2. You engaged authentically with your audience by listening to their concerns, understanding their needs, and responding empathetically and respectfully while maintaining transparency and accountability.
3. You utilized effective communication channels such as social media platforms, email newsletters, community meetings, and public events to reach your target audience.
4. Your message and platform address the most important issues impacting your community, shedding light on these issues and proposing solutions.
5. You effectively communicate your message through various channels and events, both in-person and online, in a way that inspires unity and forward movement.

Step Three: GO!

It always seems impossible until it's done.

—Nelson Mandela

Welcome to your final step where all your preparation comes to life. It is time to launch your campaign, rally support for your candidate, or champion your cause.

Nelson Mandela, the first president of South Africa and a tireless anti-apartheid activist, serves as an inspiring example. Despite facing enormous obstacles, Mandela never gave up on his cause or his country. His message of peace, justice, and freedom resonated with people around the world, demonstrating the power of a single person to effect meaningful change.

He was born in 1918 in a small village in what is now South Africa. Mandela was not afraid to be that catalyst, to stand up for what he believed in, even when it meant facing seemingly insurmountable obstacles. Despite being imprisoned for 27 years for his leadership of the African National Congress, an organization outlawed by the government for its anti-apartheid actions and positions, Mandela refused to give up on his cause and his country. He knew that his struggle was his people's, as his people's struggle was his. But Mandela opened that struggle and his message of justice to the world. His life is a reminder that no matter how daunting the task may seem, with determination, courage, and collective action, you can achieve your goals and effect meaningful change.

Now, it is your turn to make a difference. The next chapters will guide you through the process of organizing a movement, getting out the vote, and reviewing your results. Every step of this journey is an opportunity to learn, grow, and make a difference in your community.

- **Organize your community:** Build a movement and mobilize your supporters to act. Use a combination of phone banking, texting, barnstorming rallies, and events.
- **Get out the vote:** Implement your plan to encourage voter turnout. Pay attention to early voters who vote by mail and others who make decisions in the final hours before the election. Every vote counts!
- **Count every vote:** Ensure every vote is counted fairly. After the election, review the results, reflect, and learn from your campaign, and refresh your plan.

Seven

Organize a Movement

When you see something that is not just, not fair, or not right, you have to do something. You have to say something. Make a little noise. It's time for us to get into good trouble, necessary trouble.

—John Lewis

John Robert Lewis, the son of Alabama sharecroppers was an American politician, and civil rights activist, and served in the United States House of Representatives for Georgia's 5th congressional district from 1987 until he died in 2020. Lewis was a pivotal figure in the American civil rights movement, dedicating his life to promoting freedom and equality. Born on February 21, 1940, in Troy, Alabama, Lewis grew up during a time of segregation. Inspired by Dr. Martin Luther King Jr., he felt a calling to ministry and moved to Nashville, Tennessee, to attend the American Baptist Theological Seminary.

While in Nashville, Lewis became a central figure in the civil rights movement. He participated in sit-in protests to desegregate lunch counters and challenged segregation and oppression through nonviolent protest. Despite facing violence, Lewis consistently risked his safety for the cause of justice.

Lewis was a key participant in the 1960 Nashville sit-ins, the Freedom Rides, and led the first of three Selma to Montgomery marches across the Edmund Pettus Bridge. In 1965, during a march for voting rights in Selma, Alabama, state troopers attacked peaceful demonstrators, including John Lewis, with clubs and tear gas in an incident known as Bloody Sunday. His dedication and courage continue to inspire people today.

In 1986, John Lewis was elected to the U.S. House of Representatives from an Atlanta district. His election was part of a wave of new Black lawmakers from the South, a change made possible by Lewis's relentless work to expand voting rights. During his over three decades in Congress, Lewis was a powerful legislator who provided moral and political leadership within the Democratic Party, always remembering his roots as an activist.

Every big change starts with a single step. As you explore this chapter, consider how you can use these lessons in your efforts. Whether you are starting a campaign, running for office, or advocating for a cause, these insights and best practices can help you create a movement capable of making a real difference.

As you explore this chapter, you will learn valuable lessons from Lewis and other grassroots organizers. Their experiences provide insights into how to organize your community and build a movement. Lewis's life, from his work in the civil rights movement in the 1960s to his fight to preserve democracy in the 21st century, offers a wealth of knowledge on building a successful movement. Here is what you can expect to learn next:

- **Build power with people:** Relationships are critical for building a sustainable movement. Leaders like Lewis, driven by a deep commitment to justice and equality, can inspire

others and sustain a movement. Their dedication and passion can ignite the same in others, creating a powerful force for change.
- **Train and organize:** Host events and opportunities to engage, onboard, and train people in your community in person and online with the digital ladder of engagement.
- **Build alliances:** Lewis knew that movements are built on alliances. You will learn strategies for identifying key stakeholders and building relationships.
- **Mobilize support:** From sit-ins to Freedom Rides to political campaigns, Lewis inspired support and action.
- **Be resilient in the face of setbacks:** Lewis faced numerous setbacks and challenges but never stopped fighting on his journey. You will need to stay strong and keep pushing forward, even when things seem tough.

Organize a People-Powered Movement

You have defined your purpose, created your plan, formed your team, and crafted your message and story, it is time to recruit, onboard, train, and scale your base of supporters and volunteer leaders to build and scale your people-powered movement.

Community organizing is all about building trust and encouraging collective action for a common cause. This is especially crucial when working with marginalized communities, who may have low trust in the system. The success of the progressive movement hinges on gaining their trust and creating a democracy that benefits everyone.

Your best practice for sustainable community organizing is to transform people-powered actions and resources to create enduring change.

- **Share stories:** Develop a compelling narrative that explains why you are called to lead, the community you hope to mobilize, and why action is necessary.
- **Build relationships:** Establish intentional relationships as the foundation of purposeful collective actions.
- **Empower teams:** Create a distributed organizing structure that distributes power and responsibility and prioritizes all leaders rather than top-down centers of control.
- **Reimagine possibilities:** Transform resources into the power to achieve vision and clear strategic goals.
- **Act:** Measure, motivate, and drive action.

★Success Story Profile: Marshall Ganz★

Marshall Ganz, a respected community organizer and scholar, highlights the need to form strong relationships with people in communities for successful and sustainable organizing.

Ganz created a social action framework focusing on the heart (story), the head (strategy), and the hands (action). This approach, translating values into action, building relationships, collaborative leadership, strategic thinking, and turning commitments into results, has played a key role in many successful campaigns.

According to Ganz, success goes beyond immediate goals; it involves people and uplifts communities. This highlights the essence of grassroots organizing—building relationships, fostering community engagement, and empowering individuals for change. Each campaign contributes to a broader movement by strengthening networks, promoting active participation, and nurturing a shared sense of purpose.

Inspire and Develop Leaders

Identifying and organizing leaders is a crucial step in any grassroots movement. Leaders are the backbone of any movement, providing guidance, inspiration, and direction. Good organizers understand the importance of not going it alone. They require strong relationships and a team of respected people who can lead. In organizing, democracy is power, and your campaign will always be stronger if people feel their voices are represented through it.

Leadership is a continuous learning experience; anyone can become a leader. It involves skills such as active listening and building trust. However, someone who starts as a leader can easily lose trust. Effective leaders possess knowledge about community needs, along with good listening skills, compassion, honesty, courage, and the ability to inspire collective action.

Reach out and have conversations with people in your community. These conversations should feel natural. You might not cover all these points in every conversation, but it is always important to understand what the other person cares about. Practicing these conversations can be helpful. Try role-playing with a friend or teammate to get comfortable with this structure.

Reflect on your conversations. Did you listen more than you talked? How often did you make a statement when you could have asked a question? These reflections can help you improve your organizing conversations.

To inspire new leaders, it's essential to create opportunities for growth and leadership within your organization. Encourage members to take on responsibilities and tasks that challenge them and help them develop new skills. Provide mentorship and support to those who show potential for leadership. Celebrate their successes and help them learn from their mistakes. Remember, a leader isn't born but made, and your organization can be the perfect place for new leaders to emerge and flourish.

 **Tip**

> Organizing conversations can help you connect with others and understand their concerns. Here's a simple way to structure these conversations:
>
> 1. **Make introductions**: Share who you are and what you're concerned about.
>
> 2. **Identify issues**: Find out what matters to the other person.
>
> 3. **Explore the situation**: Discuss why the situation is unfair.
>
> 4. **Plan to win**: Explain why collective action is needed and outline the plan.
>
> 5. **Prepare**: Prepare for potential responses from those in power.
>
> 6. **Encourage action**: Encourage the other person to act.

Engage Supporters in the Ladder of Engagement

You will need to find people to join you, onboard, and train them with resources and support to build your base create more volunteer leaders, strong collaborations, and alliances, and sustain your movement over time.

The *"ladder of engagement"* is a powerful tool for grassroots campaigns, providing a structured pathway to transform casual supporters into dedicated activists. It begins with raising awareness about the cause or campaign, sparking interest in potential supporters. You can create interest both in person and online through various channels like social media, email campaigns, and community events. After initial interest is raised, the next step is to encourage deeper engagement. This can be done by inviting supporters to participate in activities such as volunteering, attending meetings, or making donations. The goal is to cultivate these supporters into leaders within the movement, who can then recruit and engage new supporters, creating a self-sustaining cycle of growth. The ladder of engagement outlines the progressive steps a person takes to become more involved.

- **Observers:** Shows interest and learn more through various channels, including social media and events.

- **Followers:** Agrees to receive information and engages with communications.

- **Endorsers:** Take actions like signing petitions, making small donations, or sharing content.

- **Contributors:** Make significant contributions of time, money, or social capital, such as joining a group, attending events, or making large donations.

- **Owners:** Makes ongoing, collaborative actions and major investments, often blurring the lines between themselves and the campaign. This could involve publishing about the campaign, public speaking, or deep volunteer involvement.

- **Leaders:** Become an active leader, focusing on training others, organizing others, recruiting donors, or serving on the board.

Distribute Power to Scale

People power can scale and sustain the movement most effectively when distributed across the grassroots organization without a single central point of control or failure. This approach encourages people to step up and lead independently with local autonomy, knowledge, and relationships. Big organizing involves mobilizing large numbers of volunteers to work towards a common goal.

The leadership is distributed, with no one person or group holding all the power. Responsibility is shared and sustainable, with a flat structure to create mutual accountability. You can think of it as a network of people and interconnected teams working together to further common goals. Unlike a top-down structure, this approach is flatter with more sharing of roles, resources, and responsibilities. Everyone is responsible for identifying, recruiting, and developing leaders, creating a cycle of leadership development. With distributed organizing, grassroots movements can organize and grow to scale rapidly, sustain momentum, and adapt quickly when necessary making them powerful tools for social change.

To build a people-powered movement, start by identifying people who share your purpose, values, and goals. This can start small with meetings and events but should continue over time to build power through awareness, education, activism, and opportunity moments.

Relationships are strongest when people meet in person.

Schedule regular in-person meetings and invite people from your email contact list, your website, and social media channels. Be sure to plan your meeting agenda with specific roles for meeting attendees.

Sharing stories is a crucial part of community organizing. These real stories generate emotional connections and shared values. Whether you're running a small local campaign or a large national movement, these steps will guide you through the process of organizing a movement for change.

Unlike big money-sponsored campaigns, grassroots organizing brings together people as the primary resource to fuel the campaign, candidate, or cause. You will need to inspire leaders to organize and act in your community, focus on an issue, campaign, candidate, or cause, and mobilize people to advocate for change and sustain a movement over the long term to achieve change.

Your goal is to move from a conversation to a network of people power. Community organizing and movement building are about building trust with people who share a common purpose, a commitment to action, and sustaining change over time to achieve the goal.

Volunteer engagement is crucial to harness the diverse skills, creativity, and energy of people in your community to extend your reach and impact. Every volunteer brings unique value and can play a significant role. Relationships with people who are driven by a deep commitment to your cause, like John Lewis was to justice and equality, are key to building and sustaining a movement.

Building a successful campaign involves talking to people you know - your friends, family, peers, and coworkers - and starting conversations with people in your communities about your grassroots movement. Listen to what matters to them and connect through sharing your stories. These conversations can happen anywhere: at a busy bus stop, at the farmer's market, outside of a grocery store, at the park, or in line for an event.

Identify potential volunteers, create a volunteer application, provide training, and communicate regularly. Respect and appreciate your volunteers and make them feel like they're part of your team. Volunteers are the heart of a people-powered movement.

 Tip

> The process of recruiting and integrating volunteers is key to building a successful campaign. Volunteers are the heart of any movement. It is important to respect them, value their contributions, and make them feel like they are an integral part of your team. Here are some steps to help you:
>
> 1. **Identify potential volunteers:** Start by looking for potential volunteers among your friends, family, neighbors, and colleagues. Reach out to community groups, schools, and other organizations that align with your cause.
>
> 2. **Create a volunteer application:** Develop a simple volunteer application form to collect information about your volunteers' skills, interests, and availability. This will help you match volunteers with suitable roles and tasks.
>
> 3. **Provide training:** Equip your volunteers with the skills and knowledge they need to contribute effectively to your campaign. This could include training on your

campaign's goals and strategies, communication skills, and specific tasks or roles.

4. **Communicate regularly:** Keep your volunteers informed and engaged by communicating regularly. This could include sending updates via email or social media, holding regular meetings, and providing feedback and recognition.

Engage, Onboard, and Train

Organize events and create opportunities to engage, onboard, and train people in your community, both in person and online using the digital ladder of engagement.

A best practice is to host events, whether in person or online. Success hinges on the details, so every step — from planning to follow-up — contributes to building a successful campaign. When organizing an event, consider the following resources and plan for a successful organizing meeting.

- **Plan:** Choose a suitable location, time, and date for your event. Consider public places in your community with high foot traffic or upcoming public events. Ensure the venue is accessible, with public transit availability and ADA compliance.
- **Promote:** Personally invite people and promote the event on social media, email, website, and calendar to schedule registrations. Acknowledge people as they RSVP.
- **Prepare:** Plan your meeting agenda with slides and a script for your host and guest speakers, frequently asked questions

(FAQ) for attendees, and a digital enrollment system for ongoing communications and collaboration. Have both paper and digital printable literature available as handouts. Send reminders to your RSVPs.

- **Arrange roles and logistics:** Plan your meeting agenda with specific roles for people to register attendance, check in, and capture names, phone numbers, and email contacts. Ensure your meeting location has chairs, tables, and audio/visual support.
- **Bring name tags and refreshments**: A good best practice is to have name tags for existing members and guests. Providing refreshments and potluck snacks can support the meet and greet as people arrive.
- **Help your hosts:** Arrive early if hosting at a venue. Follow your host agenda and script to help everyone get started and commit to the next steps. Use a sign-in sheet or an online platform to register attendees for ongoing communications.
- **Share stories:** The hosts and guest speakers should share their personal stories to create relationships, build your community, and create power. Sharing real stories of people generates emotional connections with shared values and feelings. This is a crucial aspect of community organizing.
- **Educate and provide organizing tools**: Provide an organizing one-pager with a link to a short video for ongoing learning. Have both paper and digital printable literature available as handouts.
- **Sign up your volunteers**: Prepare sign-up sheets for the next canvass, tabling event, or phone banking session.
- **Followup after your event:** Submit your sign-in and sign-up sheets, mark attendance on your event page, follow up

with guests about the next steps, and post any photos from your event.

★Success Story Profile: Democratic Socialists of America★

The Democratic Socialists of America (DSA) members are dedicated to building progressive movements for social change while establishing an openly socialist presence in American communities and politics.

DSA local chapters organize in their communities by building bonds of mutual trust with other people committed to social justice. The goal inspires and empowers comrades and collective power to sustain the work in the struggle for a better world. This best practice emphasizes the importance of "one-on-one" conversations, education, and action.

1. Start the conversation: sound confident, be reasonable, and be considerate. Talk about when you realized you were a democratic socialist.
2. Get them talking, then practice active listening: what kinds of issues are they interested in? What makes them question the dominant ideology? When did they realize they wanted to do something to change things? Get them talking about themselves.
3. Educate and "agitate": provide information about DSA, our goals, and what you'd like to do that would address some of the issues that they mentioned as motivating them. Talk about why they need to get involved.
4. Assess their support: can you tell if they're intrigued or scared? Ask them straight up: will you help me start a DSA

local? (or will you help plan a labor solidarity campaign? or will you come to this public forum or demonstration? etc.).
5. Move them to action and get a commitment: if they say they will help in some way, ask them to take a specific action. Take into consideration their time constraints and skills and make your "ask" big or small accordingly. Then offer an alternative (attending a local planning meeting, attending an event, putting up posters, etc.). How much time can they give to DSA? What other resources can they offer?
6. Persist in talking to another person, and another; you may need to talk to dozens of people to find five who want to organize a local.

Organize on a Budget

It is not about the size of the budget but the creativity and passion behind your organizing efforts. Tailor these ideas to fit your campaign's personality and community context, and watch the momentum build without breaking the bank.

 Tip

> Running a campaign on a shoestring budget can be challenging, but with a dash of creativity, you can make a big impact. Here are five budget-friendly ideas to organize effectively:
>
> 1. **Source discount store organizing kits:** Head to your local discount dollar store to purchase and assemble a cost-effective organizing kit for volunteers. Grab essentials like clipboards, pens, markers, poster boards, and

more. You will be surprised at the quality and variety of items available, helping you stay organized without breaking the bank.
2. **Build social media:** Build a strong social media strategy. Leverage free platforms to connect with your audience, share updates, and mobilize supporters. Craft engaging content, host virtual events, and utilize targeted advertising to maximize your online presence.
3. **Organize in your community:** Host fun events at community hotspots like farmers' markets and public transportation hubs. Create a lively atmosphere where people can rally, sign petitions, and engage with your cause. These locations provide a cost-effective way to reach a diverse audience.
4. **Create a video story series:** Craft a compelling video story series featuring individuals sharing why your campaign, candidate, or cause is vital in their lives. Personal narratives resonate deeply and can be shared across social media platforms, amplifying your message with authenticity.
5. **Do it-yourself campaign swag:** Create eye-catching buttons, stickers, and artwork that represent your campaign. Post them strategically at coffee shops, libraries, and community centers where your target audience frequents. DIY swag not only promotes your cause but also sparks conversations.
6. **Celebrate:** Host affordable victory celebrations that bring people together for a good cause. Consider activities like watching a film, reading a book, or other communal

> experiences that foster a sense of unity and purpose. These events serve as both a celebration and an opportunity to strategize for the future.

Scale with Digital

Organizing is most powerful when you engage one person at a time. To scale from a small group of individuals to a growing grassroots movement to a large scale you need to build power with organizing tools and tactics to reach many people and deliver the right message to the right person at the right time.

Digital tools are essential for organizing your community and building a movement. They can amplify your efforts, extend your reach, and potentially connect with millions of people in a short time. These tools can be used to fundraise, mobilize, and engage supporters, and organize followers. They can help you communicate with your supporters, mobilize them for events, raise funds, and automate your advocacy efforts with features for email automation, mobile messaging, petitions, events, fundraising, and advocacy automation.

However, your digital strategy should prioritize people and processes over specific digital technology. It should be flexible, adaptable, and designed to empower the people in your community and movement. For grassroots organizers, this philosophy highlights the importance of human connection, clear communication, and efficient processes. It's not just about using the latest digital tools, but about harnessing the power of people and effective processes to drive change. Explore resources available from organizations providing digital tools, resources, and best practices.

- **Nonprofit Technology Enterprise Network (NTEN):** NTEN is a community of nonprofit professionals that advocates for the strategic and equitable use of technology. They offer resources, training, and a platform for collaboration to help individuals excel in their roles and contribute to their cause. NTEN envisions a world where technology is skillfully used to drive successful missions and movements.
- **Nonprofit Tech for Good:** Technology resource for nonprofits that provides news and resources related to digital marketing and fundraising for nonprofit professionals. It offers certificate programs, guides, reports, and free or low-cost webinars.
- **Social Movement Technologies (SMT):** Non-profit organization that partners with campaigners and activists globally to foster justice in the digital age. They offer organizing strategy, training, and campaign support and have trained staff from over 4900 groups and unions. SMT is committed to supporting struggles against harmful systems and upholding values of justice for all. is a non-profit organization that collaborates with campaigners and activists worldwide to build a people-powered movement for justice in the digital age.

Plan Your Calendar of Events

Each event, whether in-person or virtual, needs a detailed plan that includes all aspects before, during, and after the event. Focus on learning and continuous improvement. After each event, work with your team to understand what worked and identify areas for improvement. This will help you continuously improve your events and make them more effective over time. This plan should include:

- **Assign a volunteer leader or captain**: Designate someone to supervise the event.
- **Scope your resources and budget**: Assess your available resources and set a spending limit.
- **Plan event details**: Decide on the event location, promotion strategy, and whether to use flyers or other materials.

 Tip

Effective organizing involves reaching your target audience with the right message at the right time. Here are some strategies and best practices for organizing both in-person and digitally:

1. **Canvass in-person:** This involves going door-to-door to engage with potential supporters. Use a script that categorizes responses as 'yes', 'no', or 'maybe' to help track support and follow-up actions.

2. **Organize digitally:** This includes sending action alerts via email or text messages, engaging supporters through social media, and using phone banking to reach a wider audience.

3. **Map with software:** Utilize mapping software to automate and scale your outreach efforts. This can help you identify key areas of support and focus your resources effectively.

4. **Organize relationships:** This strategy involves le-

veraging personal relationships to mobilize support. Encourage supporters to reach out to their networks to spread your message.

5. **Narrate stories:** Sharing personal stories can be a powerful tool for organizing. These stories can help highlight the importance of your cause and motivate others to participate.

6. **Write letters to the editor:** This can be a powerful way to reach a wider audience and shape public opinion.

7. **Host events:** Events can be a great way to engage supporters, spread your message, and mobilize action. Consider hosting a 'weekend of action' or other event to rally support.

8. **Choose the right digital tools:** Selecting the right digital tools is crucial. A good Constituent Relationship Management (CRM) tool can help you understand your audience, track trends in their support, and build a data-driven strategy for grassroots power.

9. **Create a sense of urgency and inspire action:** Be bold and take the initiative to make a difference.

Seize the Moment to Build Your Movement

Moments don't just happen; you must seize them. Grassroots organizers can harness the power of strategic moments to create impactful experiences that mobilize support and propel their movements.

A successful organizing strategy remains adaptable, identifying crucial moments and generating concrete opportunities for meaningful change. In these examples, agile strategies and tactics empower grassroots organizers to seize strategic moments, creating awareness and attention that contribute to lasting change.

- **Environmental advocacy:** Every year, protesters gather outside the Chevron Richmond Refinery to draw attention to irreversible environmental damage. This moment, strategically timed before Chevron's annual stockholder meeting, confronts the company's impact on the environment. Grassroots organizers mobilized the Richmond community to demand better environmental standards and regulations, pressuring the city council for stricter oversight of Chevron's operations.

- **Affordable housing:** Local developers, driven by profit interests, hold significant power through property ownership and capital. To address housing affordability, community members unable to afford homes can unite for change. Organizing a citizen rally before and after city council meetings to build support for affordable housing in the community. The goal is clear: advocate for the adoption of an inclusionary zoning policy, compelling developers to include affordable units in their projects.

- **Advocating for human rights:** Discrimination against non-binary individuals persists due to discriminatory beliefs and societal norms or legal systems. Grassroots organizing can counter this by promoting acceptance and legal protections. A year-long campaign, featuring educational workshops, ally training sessions, and lobbying efforts, aims to enact a local ordinance safeguarding non-binary individuals from discrimination.

 **Tip**

> Seize the moment to build a movement. Some moments rise above the routine. They make us feel engaged, joyful, surprised, or motivated at a rally or event that energizes supporters and attracts attention. These moments can redefine our understanding of ourselves or the world and deepen our relationships with others.
>
> 1. **Make your event stand out:** Enhance your event by integrating unexpected or unique elements, such as a surprise guest speaker, an innovative protest tactic, or a captivating visual component.
>
> 2. **Deliver a speech:** Deliver a public statement that reframes an issue in a new light, sparking a shift in public opinion. Use clear, compelling messaging to convey your insights. Make sure your message is accessible and resonates with your target audience.
>
> 3. **Organize:** Host a community event or online forum to bring supporters together and create a sense of unity.
>
> 4. **Network:** Create opportunities for supporters to connect, both in person and online. This could be through social media groups, community gatherings, or joint projects.

★Success Story Profile: Trans Empowerment Project★

Jack Knoxville, who started the Trans Empowerment Project, was the first trans man to run for a political position in the Southern U.S. He was fired from his job at 35 when he began his medical transition, an event that ignited his activism. Despite the challenges, including a lack of medical support and dismissive politicians, Jack was determined to make a difference.

Jack's political campaign, though unconventional, connected with others in the trans community and shared their shared experiences. The common threads of dysphoria, depression, and isolation among the community members inspired Jack to act. His first initiative was a simple yet powerful one: a clothing swap held at an artist collective house in Knoxville.

From this humble beginning, the Trans Empowerment Project was born. Today, it has grown into one of the largest providers of direct aid for the trans community in the U.S. What started as a single clothing swap in North Knoxville, TN has become a global organization in less than seven years, a testament to the power of community, resilience, and the determination to effect change.

The Trans Empowerment Project's growth is significant. The organization's website has attracted over 10,000 visitors from more than 90 different countries. This impressive reach demonstrates the global impact of the project and its resonance with people around the world. It's a testament to the power of community and the importance of the work being done by the Trans Empowerment Project.

★Success Story Profile: Chalk Star★

Kristoffer Hellén, an activist, chalk artist, and traveler, volunteered for the Bernie Sanders presidential campaigns and fostered relationships with people through creativity and street chalk art. He started as a volunteer with more than 500 hours tabling for Bernie in Santa Cruz, California.

Kristoffer discovered that creating a Bernie Sanders message with chalk offered a continuous presence on the street, not just in one place, but in fifty places, or more, all at once. The first chalks, in downtown Santa Cruz and the local community college, were well received. Soon, he was traveling around California and the country sparking conversations with people from college students to people in communities eager to learn more.

The Chalk Activist seized the moment to begin the journey with a single purpose - to chalk Bernie Sanders' name at as many places as possible across California, the country, and around the world.

- **Inspire with art**: The chalk messages demonstrate the power of a well-crafted message in inspiring action on a crucial issue.
- **Effective use of physical space**: The chalk messages effectively used physical space to amplify the campaign message, demonstrating the power of a well-crafted message in inspiring action on a crucial issue.
- **Community engagement**: The chalk messages sparked numerous conversations among the students and the community, demonstrating the power of grassroots activism in raising awareness and driving a movement.

★*Success Story Profile: BART for Jovanka*★

Jovanka Beckles has dedicated her life to public service. She is a vocal advocate for the working class, the poor, the unhoused, and those at risk of incarceration. Her policy achievements include banning the box on city job applications, providing local identification cards, fighting for rent control, and raising the minimum wage. She served on the Richmond City Council and the AC Transit Board, delivering results for her city, two counties, transit riders, and transit workers.

The "BART for Jovanka" campaign was a creative organizing strategy for Jovanka Beckles' run for the California State Assembly. Volunteers, donned in campaign shirts and buttons, boarded the Bay Area Rapid Transit (BART) at various stations from Richmond to Oakland, the district Jovanka was contesting. In Oakland, volunteers disembarked with Jovanka to distribute campaign materials, effectively reaching thousands of people. This innovative approach not only raised awareness but also built power for the candidate. The campaign involved canvassing at each station from 4 pm to 6 pm, riding the BART with Jovanka, and returning to the original station to complete canvassing. This successful event exemplifies the power of community-driven action in political campaigns.

★*Success Story Profile: Mosquito Fleet*★

The Mosquito Fleet, a regional network of paddlers, sailors, and activists, is committed to climate justice and a fossil-free Pacific Northwest. Amidst a global climate crisis and the threat of our region becoming a fossil fuel superhighway, the fleet is building a bold movement that empowers local communities. Their goal is to dismantle the extractive economy by prioritizing indigenous sovereignty and protecting community and ecosystem health through creative on-water direct action and grassroots movement building.

"*Kayaktivism*" refers to the use of kayaks in protest as a strategic community-building tactic. Training programs are offered for safe and effective implementation, and resources are provided for those interested in safe water paddling and protest training in their community. This approach is also beneficial for those planning actions or seeking to enhance their community's skills. It demonstrates the power of organized, community-driven action in effecting meaningful change.

Movements in History

Organizing has played a pivotal role in driving lasting change through people-powered movements throughout history. These movements highlight the power of community organizations in creating awareness, sparking action, and maintaining momentum for lasting change. They exemplify the impact of grassroots organizing on society and underscore the ability of individuals to effect change and the importance of sustaining that change through a movement.

- **Women's Rights and Suffrage Movement:** The women's rights and suffrage movement, led by trailblazers like Susan B. Anthony and Elizabeth Cady Stanton, passionately advocated for women's right to vote.
- **Labor Unions:** Labor unions have been instrumental in championing workers' rights, emphasizing fair wages and safe working conditions.
- **Non-Violent Protest - Mahatma Gandhi's Satyagraha:** Mahatma Gandhi utilized the strategy of nonviolent protest, known as Satyagraha, leading the Indian independence movement against British rule and culminating in India's independence in 1947.
- **Civil Rights Movement:** Key figures like Martin Luther King Jr., Rosa Parks, and Malcolm X spearheaded the Civil

Rights movement, dedicated to securing equal rights for African Americans and other minority groups.
- **Occupy Wall Street:** Originating in Zuccotti Park in 2011, the Occupy Wall Street movement critiqued Wall Street, corporate America, and the super-rich.
- **Environmental Movement - Schools Strike for Climate:** The Schools Strike for Climate, also known as Fridays for Future, exerted pressure on politicians to address the pressing issue of climate change.
- **LGBTQ+ Movement:** The LGBTQ+ movement fervently advocates for equal rights and protections, irrespective of sexual orientation or gender identity.
- **Black Lives Matter:** An international initiative, the Black Lives Matter movement is committed to combating racism and anti-Black violence, notably focusing on issues such as police brutality.

Organize for Peace

Peace movements have a rich history, demonstrating the power of collective action in promoting harmony and justice. From anti-war protests to efforts fostering diplomatic solutions, these movements have left an indelible mark on our world.

★*Success Story Profile: Mahatma Gandhi*★

Mohandas Karamchand Gandhi, known as Mahatma Gandhi, was born on October 2, 1869, in Porbandar, India. He was an Indian lawyer, anti-colonial nationalist, and political ethicist who led the successful campaign for India's independence from British rule using nonviolent resistance1. His philosophy of truth-focused, non-violent non-cooperation, which he called Satyagraha, inspired movements for civil rights and freedom across the world.

Gandhi authored several influential books, including "The Story of My Experiments with Truth", "The Essential Gandhi", "Hind Swaraj or Indian Home Rule", "Third Class in Indian Railways", and "Bhagavad Gita According to Gandhi" among others. His writings have had a profound impact, providing insights into his philosophy and methods of peaceful resistance.

Gandhi's nonviolent approach to political change not only led to India's independence but also influenced other leaders around the world. One of the most notable figures influenced by Gandhi was Martin Luther King Jr., who argued that the Gandhian philosophy was "the only morally and practically sound method open to oppressed people in their struggle for freedom". King learned much about Gandhi through his writings and was heavily influenced by the Gandhian principle of non-violence in his rise to becoming a civil rights activist. Thus, Gandhi's legacy continues to inspire and guide movements for civil rights and freedom around the world.

★Success Story Profile: Daniel Ellsberg★

Daniel Ellsberg, born April 7, 1931, is an American political activist and former military analyst. He started his career in the military and academia, but his life changed dramatically when he leaked the Pentagon Papers in 1971. While working at the RAND Corporation, Ellsberg released this top-secret study of U.S. government decision-making during the Vietnam War to The New York Times, The Washington Post, and other newspapers. This act challenged the U.S. government's public justification for the war.

Ellsberg's courageous act of whistleblowing marked a significant turning point in public opinion about the Vietnam War. Despite facing charges under the Espionage Act of 1917 and other charges of theft and conspiracy, all charges against Ellsberg were dismissed due to governmental misconduct and illegal evidence-gathering. Ellsberg's legacy extends beyond his role in the Pentagon Papers controversy. He has contributed to various publications and authored several books, including an autobiography, "Secrets: A Memoir of Vietnam and the Pentagon Papers", and "The Doomsday Machine: Confessions of a Nuclear War Planner". His life and actions continue to inspire and influence discussions on government transparency and accountability.

★Success Story Profile: Roots Action★

Founded in 2011 by Norman Solomon and Jeff Cohen, RootsAction is an online initiative committed to economic fairness, equal rights, civil liberties, environmental protection, and ending endless wars. Independent of major parties, it educates and mobilizes voters on crucial issues like climate change and civil rights, challenging both Republican and Democratic policies. Endorsed by prominent progressives such as Jim Hightower, Cornel West, and Naomi Klein, RootsAction advocates for policies addressing economic, social, racial, and environmental challenges, including Medicare For All, the Green New Deal, canceling student debt, cutting the military budget, and raising the minimum wage.

RootsAction has successfully organized peaceful actions. In 2013, Norman Solomon presented a petition with over 100,000 signatures to the Nobel Committee, urging Chelsea Manning for the Nobel Peace Prize. Pioneering support for NSA whistleblower Edward Snowden, the organization continues to be a progressive force, inspiring a new generation of leaders to strive for a more equitable future. RootsAction remains a beacon of progressive change, influencing the path toward a fairer tomorrow.

Build a Strong Labor Movement

The labor movement and collective bargaining have profoundly shaped global workforces and working conditions. Originating in the late colonial period, the Federal Society of Journeymen Cordwainers in Philadelphia marked the beginning of sustained trade union organization in 1794. Throughout history, the labor movement has championed better wages, reasonable hours, safer working conditions, and the eradication of child labor. The national introduction of collective bargaining occurred in 1918 with the establishment of the War Labor Conference Board.

Despite declining unionization rates in recent decades, a resurgence in organizing activity has taken place, increasing union members. This revival is fueled by worker dissatisfaction with pay, benefits, job security, and working conditions, sparking a renewed interest in collective bargaining. In 2023, the United States witnessed a remarkable surge in labor victories and strikes, with workers resetting their expectations and demanding considerably more than in previous years. This shift has prompted numerous corporations to recalibrate their pay packages in union contracts, resulting in substantial and sometimes unprecedented settlements. Notable successes include:

- **American Airlines Pilots:** 15,000 pilots secured an impressive 46% pay increase over four years.
- **Hollywood Studios (Actors and Writers):** Hollywood actors (165,000) and writers (15,000) went on strike simultaneously, resulting in studios largely acceding to union demands on pay, minimum staffing levels, and limiting the use of artificial intelligence in scripts after nearly five months.
- **Kaiser Permanente Workers:** Following a three-day strike, 85,000 workers at Kaiser Permanente won a substantial 21%

pay increase and a $25 minimum wage for Kaiser's workers in California.
- **Los Angeles School District Workers:** A workforce of 30,000, including bus drivers, cafeteria workers, and teachers' aides, secured a significant 30% wage hike over four years.
- **MIT Graduate Student Workers:** Over 3,800 graduate student workers at MIT secured a 12.6% increase in their stipend, a $10,000 needs-based childcare subsidy, and an 84% dental subsidy.
- **Oregon Nurses at Providence Portland Hospital:** 1,400 nurses at Providence Portland Hospital in Oregon obtained raises ranging between 17% and 27% over two years.
- **UPS Teamster Members:** 340,000 Teamster members at UPS achieved raises of $7.50 an hour over five years, with drivers' pay reaching $49 an hour and part-time workers receiving a 48% pay increase on average.

These victories represent a remarkable shift in power dynamics, showcasing the growing influence of workers and unions in negotiating improved pay and benefits.

To strengthen the labor movement, consider organizing efforts in your community, workplace, or around common purposes. Engage with fellow workers, discuss shared concerns, and explore opportunities for collective action. Establishing communication channels, utilizing online platforms, and fostering a sense of solidarity can contribute to building a robust and united labor front.

★Success Story Profile: We Are Somebody★

"We Are Somebody" is a new organization dedicated to championing workers' rights across America. It is partnering with the

Amazon Labor Union and was founded by Nina Turner, a passionate advocate for workers. Turner, a former Ohio State Senator and a national surrogate for Senator Bernie Sanders, aims to amplify, celebrate, and act upon the stories of workers. The goal of "We Are Somebody" is to bring these stories to the forefront of national discourse.

The organization helps amplify the narrative of striking workers from the picket line to the public, educates non-union workers on the impact and importance of the labor movement, and supports workers in contract negotiations so they can come to the table from the strongest possible position.

Build Alliances and Partnerships

Throughout history, organizers have recognized that strong movements are founded on robust alliances and community partnerships. In your journey towards victory, the foundation for grassroots organizing and change lies in identifying stakeholders and fostering enduring relationships built on trust and commitment. Learn how alliances form the bedrock of sustainable movements, guaranteeing long-term success through shared purpose and collective action.

★*Success Story Profile: Winning Richmond*★

"Winning Richmond: How a Progressive Alliance Won City Hall" narrates the inspiring story of a grassroots progressive alliance that transformed Richmond, California, a city long dominated by the massive Chevron oil refinery, into an award-winning "Green & Clean" community.

Instrumental in this transformation was the Richmond Progressive Alliance (RPA), co-founded by Gayle McLaughlin, which sought to unite the left across political parties and shift decision-making from corporations to the people. The RPA mobilized support for progressive policies, collaborating with local groups to achieve milestones such as fair rent control, a $15 minimum wage by 2020, and an ordinance preventing the city from sharing information with ICE.

Gayle McLaughlin and Jovanka Beckles are important leaders in this movement, both former Richmond City Council members who played crucial roles in challenging Chevron's influence and electing progressive candidates to city offices. McLaughlin, a former educator and activist, served two terms as Richmond's mayor, while Beckles continues her advocacy as a candidate for California State Senate. Their stories, alongside the collective efforts of the RPA, exemplify the transformative power of grassroots organizing in bringing about meaningful change.

Mobilize Support

From sit-ins to Freedom Rides to political campaigns, Lewis was a master at mobilizing support. Organizing and mobilizing, two distinct yet interconnected aspects of community engagement, are crucial for building a sustainable movement.

When organizing, the emphasis is on fostering relationships and trust within a community. This involves listening to community members, respecting diverse views, and striving for consensus. The focus is on people, their priorities, and sustaining efforts to achieve a common purpose over time.

Conversely, mobilizing is action-oriented, concentrating on moving people to act and sustaining engagement by demonstrating momentum and direction. The goal is to propel the movement forward by pushing for the next step in a sequence of actions.

Mobilizing people to take action involves employing a diverse range of tactics that resonate with various audiences. Successful strategies include organizing rallies and events to build a sense of community and shared purpose, utilizing the power of collective presence. Lobbying elected officials is an impactful tactic, leveraging direct engagement to influence policy decisions. Protesting serves as a visible and vocal method to express dissent, drawing attention to critical issues. Digital petitions harness the reach of online platforms, enabling widespread support and facilitating quick, accessible participation. Employing digital mobilization goes beyond petitions, engaging individuals to make calls to elected officials, write letters, and actively participate in advocacy efforts. These multifaceted approaches cater to different preferences and effectively mobilize diverse communities towards collective action, reinforcing the strength of grassroots movements.

 Tip

> Your representatives are there to serve you, and it is your right and responsibility to hold them accountable. This can be done by regularly contacting them, monitoring their voting records, and understanding the legislative process. Here are some ways to do this:
>
> 1. **Contact your representatives**: Reach out to express your views or ask for their support. The most effective way to reach them is through their preferred method, which could be phone calls, emails, letters, social media, or in-person meetings. You can use tools like MyReps or Democracy.io to find their contact information.
>
> 2. **Track their voting records**: Monitor how your

representatives vote on issues that matter to you. You can also see how long they have held office when they are up for reelection, and what bills they have sponsored or co-sponsored. GovTrack.us is a useful tool for this.

3. **Learn about the legislative process**: Educate yourself on how bills are passed in Congress and how you can influence the process. You can also learn about the roles and responsibilities of different branches and levels of government, and how they interact with each other. Congress.gov is a great resource for this.

4. **Send a message:** To influence your local, state, or federal representatives on an issue or bill, write them a letter. State your position, provide supporting facts, and express the impact on your community. Request their stance and thank them for their attention.

Resilience in the Face of Setbacks

Lewis faced numerous setbacks and challenges but never stopped fighting on his journey. You will also need to be resilient and keep moving forward, even when the odds seem stacked against you. It is very important to adopt a resilient mindset.

- Embrace setbacks as opportunities for learning and growth, understanding that challenges can fuel innovation and adaptation.

- Cultivate a strong support network within your organizing

community, fostering a collective resilience that enables individuals to lean on each other during tough times.

- Maintain an unwavering commitment to your cause, acknowledging that persistence in the face of adversity is the driving force behind lasting change.

Chapter Checklist: Organize a Movement

In this chapter, you explored the art of community organizing, learning how to mobilize power to effect change. Community organizing requires a sustained commitment to build your movement. Success hinges on a clear understanding of your mission, a well-defined plan, and the ability to mobilize and sustain your movement. Here is a summary of the key points:

Checklist:

1. You have empowered your community by putting people at the heart of your efforts and transforming communities into constituencies committed to a common purpose.
2. You practiced organizing strategies such as public narrative, relationship building, team structuring, strategizing, and action, which were critical for building a movement.
3. You discovered and engaged supporters by funneling them through engagement phases and training leadership to high levels of power.
4. You mobilized action by focusing on power dynamics and using digital tools to mobilize your people both in person and online, building scale and power over time.
5. You sustained your movement by understanding the importance of long-term effort, as real change can take years or even decades to achieve.

Eight

Get Out the Vote

Someone struggled for your right to vote. Use it.
—*Susan B. Anthony*

Susan B. Anthony, a pivotal figure in the women's suffrage movement, was born into a Quaker family committed to social equality. At 17, she was already collecting anti-slavery petitions. Her lifelong friend and co-worker in social reform activities, Elizabeth Cady Stanton, joined her in founding the New York Women's State Temperance Society after Anthony was prevented from speaking at a conference because of her gender.

Their collaboration continued through the Civil War with the Women's Loyal National League, which conducted the largest petition drive in U.S. history at that time, collecting nearly 400,000 signatures in support of abolishing slavery. Post-war, they initiated the American Equal Rights Association, campaigning for equal rights for both women and African Americans.

In 1868, they began publishing a women's rights newspaper called The Revolution and a year later founded the National Woman Suffrage Association. This organization eventually merged with its rival to form the National American Woman Suffrage Association, with Anthony as its driving force.

In 1872, she dared to challenge the system. She was arrested for voting, an act that was considered illegal because she was a woman, and only men had the right to vote at that time. Despite being convicted in a trial that caught the nation's attention, she stood her ground and refused to pay the fine. The authorities, surprisingly, did not take any further action against her. Six years later, in 1878, Anthony, along with her ally Stanton, took a bold step towards equality. They presented an amendment to Congress, advocating for women's right to vote. This proposal would later be known as the Susan B. Anthony Amendment.

However, it wasn't until 1920, long after Anthony's time, that this amendment was finally ratified as the Nineteenth Amendment to the U.S. Constitution. This marked a significant milestone in the fight for gender equality, granting women the right to vote. Anthony's courage and determination continue to inspire us today, reminding us of the power of standing up for what we believe in.

Anthony tirelessly campaigned for women's suffrage, giving up to 100 speeches per year and working on many state campaigns. She also played a key role in creating the International Council of Women and helped bring about the World's Congress of Representative Women at the World's Columbian Exposition in Chicago in 1893.

Despite initial ridicule and accusations of trying to destroy marriage, the public perception of Anthony changed dramatically during her lifetime. Her 80th birthday was celebrated in the White House at President William McKinley's invitation. She became the first female citizen depicted on U.S. coinage when her portrait appeared on the 1979 dollar coin.

In the spirit of Susan B. Anthony, a tireless advocate for democracy and women's suffrage, this chapter delves into the crucial step of getting out the vote. Anthony once said, "*Someone struggled for your right to vote. Use it.*" Now more than ever, it is crucial that we not only vote but inspire others to do the same. We are at a key point in history, and every vote counts. Drawing from the best practices of successful organizations and candidates, you will be equipped with the tools and knowledge necessary to run a successful campaign. Every vote matters, and you can make a real difference. This chapter will guide you to:

- **Implement a phased voter turnout plan:** Learn how to create an effective plan to encourage voter turnout. This includes strategies for targeting voters and promoting the candidate effectively. Understand the different phases of your election campaign, plan your campaign calendar for peak moments, and impact before, during, and after critical election dates.
- **Get elected with a limited budget:** Explore how to build a winning campaign with limited resources using volunteers, a strong message, endorsements, door-knocking strategies, and digital strategies.
- **Organize voter registration drives**: Understand the importance of voter registration and learn how to organize effective registration drives.
- **Gain visibility:** Learn how to use yard signs, events, rallies, and debates to increase your visibility in the district.
- **Earn endorsements:** Find out how to earn endorsements and support from grasstop leaders, influencers, grassroots supporters, alliances, and voters.
- **Target likely voters and precincts:** Understand how to identify and target likely voters and key precincts.
- **Engage prospective voters across channels**: Discover

how to use various channels, both offline and online, to remind people to vote. This includes exploring the potential of digital tools to reach a wider audience.
- **Remind people to vote:** Learn how to use various channels effectively to remind people to vote.
- **Enjoy the journey:** Stay focused on your message, have fun, and whether you win or lose, you are part of our history and a role model for future generations.

Implement a Voter Engagement Plan

Deciding to run for office is a big step that needs careful planning. Before launching, you will need to take these first steps to get started:

- **Register for the election:** Start by officially registering as a candidate. This usually means submitting paperwork to your local election office, which could include a declaration of candidacy and other forms. Make sure to check the specific requirements and deadlines in your area.
- **Collect signatures for your election petition:** In many places, you will need to collect a certain number of signatures from registered voters to appear on the ballot. This process, known as petitioning, is a great way to start engaging with potential supporters.
- **Build your campaign team:** Put together a team of dedicated people who can help manage different parts of your campaign, like fundraising, communications, and coordinating volunteers. Your team will be instrumental in implementing your campaign strategy.
- **Do the math:** Work out how many votes you will need

to win. Look at past election turnouts, demographics, and factors that could affect voter turnout.

- **Announce your campaign:** After you have prepared, it is time to officially announce your candidacy. You can do this through a public event, a press release, or a social media post. Use this opportunity to share your campaign message and vision with voters.

Tip

Running for office requires a strategic approach, grounded in a deep understanding of the electorate. You can use election data to inform your campaign strategy. Calculate the math to finalize your plan to get out the vote for your candidate and win.

1. **Understand the voters** Analyze voter data from previous elections in your district to estimate total voter count and party registration (Democrat, Republican, No Party Preference). Use demographic information like race and age to target specific voter groups.

2. **Revisit turnout in previous elections:** Review the vote counts from the previous three elections so you can estimate the number of votes needed to win. This gives you a ballpark figure for the number of votes you will need to win. General elections typically have higher turnout than primary elections and presidential election years historically have larger voter turnout overall.

3. **Finalize campaign plan, strategy, and goals:** Focus

on important issues, create coalitions with progressive grassroots organizations, and partner effectively.

4. **Engage unions and progressive organizations:** Ask for endorsements and seek support from the members of these groups to mobilize their members to participate in your campaign, support voter registration campaigns, and get out the vote.

5. **Find voters with deep canvassing**: Engage likely voters in meaningful conversations about the key issues in the community. Once you have identified a supporter, ask them to help you win and use techniques like "Vote Tripling" to engage three more voters.

6. **Target your outreach**: Reach out to specific subgroups of voters with specialized literature and media approaches.

7. **Use social media**: Prioritize social media platforms to reach younger voters.

8. **Maximize earned coverage**: Use events, and press releases on hot issues to gain media coverage.

9. **Prioritize people over profit:** The needs of people must be at the forefront. People have the power to overcome the power of corporate money. The campaign will accept no corporate contributions or contributions from PACs that work in the interests of Corporations or

> charter schools. Your key issues of campaign themes and issues should reflect this ethos.

After these initial steps, the focus of your campaign will shift toward voter engagement, which includes developing a plan to encourage voter turnout, organizing voter registration drives, and using different channels to remind people to vote. Implementing a phased voter engagement plan is crucial for a successful campaign.

Phase 1: Campaign Launch and Awareness

- Focus on building awareness for your candidacy, and engaging with volunteer supporters, donors, and endorsements.
- Deliver your candidate's message in person and through your candidate's website, email, social media, and printed materials.
- Speak at local events, rallies, meetings, and farmers' markets to win early support.
- Ask for small donations from people to take on special interest groups and not be biased with corporate contributions.
- Build an endorsement program and meet with key leaders to gain their support.
- Build your volunteer list and voter database with targeted strategies for different precincts and voter categories early in phase 1.

Phase 2: Mobilize People

- Activate your campaign team and volunteer leaders to help you spread the word with their help canvassing in person

and at key locations such as farmers markets, local neighbors events, and attending rallies and debates.
- Use effective tools like lawn signs, buttons, stickers, canvassing literature, email, web, and social media to get your message out to voters.
- Combine your in-person canvassing with phone banking and text messaging for maximum reach.

Phase 3: Get out the vote

- Focus on canvassing the likely early voters to sign them up to vote for you and volunteer for you.
- Ensure your printed materials (lawn signs, buttons, stickers, canvassing literature, email, web, and social media) are ready for this important time.
- Engage likely voters with voter tools such as Action Network, Open Field, Voter Action Network (VAN), and others.

Get Elected with a Limited Budget

Running for office with limited resources poses challenges, but it is entirely possible to build a winning campaign through strategic and resourceful approaches. As a first-time candidate, you likely will not have the luxury of campaign managers or sizable budgets, but your commitment to public service, authentic voice, and community values can be powerful assets. Many entry-level elected offices provide an excellent starting point for aspiring candidates, where the support of family, friends, and volunteers becomes the most crucial resource. Your time, dedicated to working hard at events, debates, endorsement meetings, and connecting with voters, volunteers, and donors, becomes your primary focus.

Running for office is hard work and takes a lot of effort. Every single day, you will need to talk to voters, make personal contact, and build relationships. This is the most important thing you can do. You will need to have conversations, listen, make phone calls, knock on doors, attend small meetings and events, and speak at debates. You need to be at your best. Be prepared to ask people questions and listen more than you speak. This is one of the most important things you can do. This is a job that requires a lot of hard work, but it can also be very rewarding.

As a first-time candidate for political office, the most important thing you can do is focus on the "*why.*" Why do you want to win the election? Why are you the best person to be trusted to support the interests of the people in your community that you will be representing? You need to be able to answer these questions with concise, clear, and consistent messages. You need to be able to articulate your vision for the "why" and how you have experience and solutions to the issues and problems that are facing the people in your community that you are interested in voting for you. Why should people vote for you? These are the things you want to be able to build into your story in terms of the accomplishments that you expect in your role in the elected office. You need to be very specific and rank these goals in order of what you can achieve and what your community needs from you as an elected official.

Your unique advantage lies in your personal story and a message that differentiates you from other candidates. For a first-time political candidate with a shoestring budget, elevating name recognition is a paramount priority. Introduce yourself to voters, emphasizing authenticity and shared values.

- **Start with family, friends, and neighbors:** Harness the support of those closest to you, encouraging them to spread the word and actively participate in your campaign.

- **Build on existing relationships:** Tap into your network within the community. Utilize connections from your professional and personal life to extend your reach.
- **Create digital and social media presence:** Establish and maintain a robust presence on social media platforms, sharing your message, and photo, and engaging with potential voters.
- **Host a lawn sign-making party:** Invite creative volunteers to help craft handmade campaign signs and strategically place them in high-visibility areas within the community.
- **Write letters to the editor:** Ask your volunteers to craft thoughtful letters to local newspapers, sharing your perspective on pertinent issues and subtly introducing your candidacy.
- **Campaign door-to-door:** Personally connect with constituents by walking door-to-door, engaging in meaningful conversations, and leaving a lasting impression.
- **Participate in events:** Attend all rallies, debates, tall halls, and relevant community gatherings such as farmers' markets and parades to maximize exposure and interact with a diverse audience.
- **Plan media coverage:** Seek visibility in local newspapers through letters to the editor and garner endorsements to boost credibility.

You must prioritize carefully with a limited budget. Focus on critical areas that guarantee maximum visibility. Invest in compelling photos and videos that convey your message, and image, and reference your website and social media channels. Begin by recruiting volunteers to form a dedicated campaign team, organizing house parties, and engaging in door-knocking, phone calls, and letter-writing campaigns to build awareness and support. Be persistent, work diligently each day, and strategically ramp up efforts leading to the first ballots, ensuring a strong finish on election day. Remember, resilience and consistent effort are your allies in building widespread awareness and securing voter support.

With limited resources, door-to-door canvassing becomes a key tactic for connecting with voters directly and seeking their support. Gaining endorsements and preparing for high-visibility events such as town halls and debates should be strategic priorities as they contribute significantly to building credibility and visibility leading up to the election.

To maximize impact, leverage digital strategies strategically, utilizing social media platforms to amplify your message, connect with constituents, and mobilize grassroots support. Remember, success lies not in the size of your budget but in the authenticity of your engagement and the resonance of your message with the community you want to serve.

 Tip

Running for office on a limited budget? Creativity and resourcefulness can often outshine a hefty budget. Tailor these ideas to fit your campaign's unique personality and community context for maximum impact. Here are five creative ideas to make the most impact without breaking the bank:

1. **Connect personally:** Reach out to your immediate circle—family, friends, neighbors, and colleagues. Personally ask for their support, votes, and any assistance they

can provide. Building a grassroots movement often starts with those closest to you.

2. **Build your list:** Create a comprehensive contact list with names, emails, and phone numbers of people you know. Invite them to join your email list and be part of your campaign's inner circle. Leverage the power of personal connections and word-of-mouth.

3. **Tap into creativity:** Identify the creative minds in your network—artists, writers, and community leaders. Ask for their help in crafting compelling campaign messages, visuals, and engagement strategies. Creative input can go a long way in making your campaign stand out.

4. **Host volunteer events:** Organize volunteer events with engaging activities. Have volunteers assist in creating campaign signs through arts and crafts. Capture photos and videos for your campaign site and social media. Fun activities not only save costs but also foster a sense of community.

5. **Seek support:** Reach out to organizations aligned with your issues. Approach local progressive clubs, environmental groups, unions, and other like-minded organizations. Seek endorsements, donations, or volunteer support. Leverage their existing networks to amplify your message.

Campaign Committee Roles

Whether you are a first-time candidate new to politics or a seasoned incumbent seeking re-election, you should plan the structure and roles of your support team.

Your campaign committee is the backbone of your electoral journey, influencing your ability to secure victory. You can form your team with a combination of dedicated volunteers, friends, family members, or experienced staff and consultants. Reach out to your community early in the process to recruit support from experienced and enthusiastic individuals from various organizations, unions, and volunteer networks who can significantly contribute to your campaign committee.

Your success relies on promptly establishing this team, fostering a collaborative culture, and defining clear roles, goals, and norms to guide your collective efforts seamlessly through all phases of the campaign. You will need to find people to take on several important roles. Each role is crucial to the success of the campaign, and volunteers in these positions can make a significant impact on the campaign's outcome.

- **Plan events and house parties:** Organize and host gatherings to spread awareness about the campaign and engage potential supporters.
- **Coordinate volunteers:** Recruit, manage, and coordinate volunteers for various campaign activities.
- **Distribute campaign lit:** Distribute informational pamphlets about the campaign in public spaces or door-to-door.
- **Engage with press and media:** Act as the primary point of contact for media inquiries, and represent the campaign in interviews and press conferences.
- **Write stories, content, and graphics:** Create and distribute

written content such as press releases, newsletters, and blog posts to inform the public about campaign updates. Design visual content for the campaign, including logos, banners, and social media graphics.
- **Amplify on social media:** Manage the campaign's social media presence, engage with followers, and spread the campaign message online.
- **Raise funds for your election:** Organize fundraising events and initiatives to finance the campaign.
- **Manage data:** Analyze campaign data to inform strategy and decision-making.
- **Organize a phone bank:** Make calls to potential voters to inform them about the campaign and encourage voter turnout.
- **Distribute signs:** Coordinate the distribution of campaign signs to supporters and public spaces.
- **Manage endorsements:** Manage relationships with individuals and organizations that endorse the campaign.
- **Consult on political strategy:** Oversee the campaign's political strategy and liaise with political partners.

Planning is essential for a successful campaign. Create a calendar that covers all the important aspects of your get-out-the-voter plan, start by working backward from the election day, and mark the key dates and deadlines. Next, plan events, activities, and goals that match your campaign strategy. Here are some things you should add to your calendar:

- **Election Day:** This is the most crucial day of your campaign. Ensure you have enough volunteers, materials, and transportation to get your supporters to the voting locations.

- **Voter registration deadline:** This is the last day for eligible voters to register or update their registration. Use this date to motivate potential voters to register.
- **Absentee ballot application deadline:** This is the last day for voters who want to vote by mail to request an absentee ballot. Remind your supporters to apply for an absentee ballot if they can't vote in person.
- **Ballot receipt deadline:** All ballots, whether mailed or in person, must be received by election officials by this date. Use this as a final push to get your supporters to return their ballots as soon as possible.
- **Mail-in ballot application deadline:** This is the last day for voters who want to receive a ballot by mail to apply for one. Inform your supporters about the option of voting by mail and how to do it.
- **Debates, town halls, and candidate forums:** These are crucial opportunities for the candidates to share their ideas with voters. The dates for these events can change, so keep an eye on local event schedules. Use these events to show off your candidate's strengths, emphasize your campaign's message, and rally your supporters.
- **Monthly deadlines for donation goals:** Set monthly fundraising goals and track your progress towards these goals. Consistent fundraising is vital for a successful campaign. Use these deadlines to inspire your donors, show appreciation to your contributors, and celebrate your successes. Consistent fundraising is key to a successful campaign.
- **Endorsements:** Securing endorsements from influential figures or organizations can significantly boost your campaign's credibility. Start connecting with potential endorsers early in your campaign. These endorsements can help attract

more supporters, get more media coverage, and gather more resources.
- **Volunteers and canvassing goals:** Volunteers are the heart of your campaign. They can assist with tasks like phone banking, door knocking, text messaging, and social media. Set weekly or daily goals for your volunteers and canvassing activities. You can use these goals as a way to recruit more volunteers, train them, and recognize them.

Encourage Voter Registration

Strategies that encourage people to register to vote and also to create a voting plan are important to turn out the vote on election day. Hosting volunteer registration tables at farmers' markets, college campuses, and public transportation areas are great place for face-to-face interactions, providing individuals with the opportunity to register on the spot and receive information on crafting a personalized voting plan.

Have fun and set up a weekly or daily volunteer team that schedules a table and information booth for people riding on buses, trains, and public transportation for their daily commute. This helps ensure widespread visibility and accessibility, prompting individuals to consider their voting options while commuting. Be ready with signs, banners, and signup information for the election process. Make it fun and smile or create some entertainment with music and songs to get attention and interest. These direct engagement tactics, coupled with an online presence and social media campaigns, create a comprehensive approach to reach diverse demographics and motivate them to engage in the electoral process.

★Success Story Profile: League of Women Voters★

The League of Women Voters is dedicated to voter education and engagement and exemplifies effective strategies for boosting voter participation. Through their presence at farmers' markets, community fairs, and public transportation hubs, they successfully registered voters, distributed educational materials, and encouraged individuals to create voting plans. By leveraging social media platforms, they have amplified their reach and provided easily accessible resources for potential voters. The League's commitment to inclusive and widespread civic participation serves as a beacon, demonstrating that a combination of community engagement, online initiatives, and targeted outreach can significantly impact voter registration, planning, and turnout.

Create Awareness

Your most important priority in the early stages of your campaign should be to raise awareness. Concentrate your efforts on high-visibility tactics to reach volunteers and voters as soon as possible. Your goal is to make your campaign as visible as possible to attract and retain supporters.

1. **Campaign materials**: Create campaign literature, signs, banners, buttons, stickers, and digital assets featuring your name, high-resolution photo, website, and campaign slogan. This helps build face and name recognition for your campaign.
2. **Yard signs**: Distribute yard signs with your message to enhance your visibility.
3. **Events and rallies**: Plan and participate in community events and rallies to connect directly with voters. These

engagements foster personal connections and can generate media coverage, contributing to heightened visibility.
4. **Debates**: Leverage debates to showcase your knowledge, ideas, and commitment to the community. A strong debate performance can significantly increase your profile among voters.
5. **Digital presence**: Maintain a strong online presence across various social media platforms. Regular updates about your campaign activities can keep your audience engaged and informed.

Earn Endorsements

Reach out to community leaders and organizations that provide an endorsement process for the elected office. You will need to demonstrate yourself as a candidate based on your position on the issues, experience, values, and trusted relationships. These endorsements are valuable for sharing on your campaign website, email list, and social media as well as to build credibility for your campaign during debates and speaking event opportunities. Ask for help from these organizations to support your campaign with volunteers to win the election.

- **Progressive organization leaders:** Develop relationships with influential grasstop leaders who can vouch for your candidacy. Their endorsement adds credibility and can sway undecided voters.
- **Grassroots supporters:** Cultivate support from grassroots activists and supporters who can champion your cause at the grassroots level, helping to build a broad base of advocates.
- **Alliances and voters:** Form alliances with like-minded

organizations and individuals, securing their endorsements and support. Engage with voters directly to build a groundswell of enthusiasm.

Organize Volunteers to Get Out the Vote

Organizing volunteer canvassing is a crucial part of getting out the vote. It relies on volunteer leaders to host and recruit volunteers for voter contact events such as canvasses, phone banks, and voter registration drives. Plan your candidate canvassing volunteer event

One tactic stands out as the most impactful for securing victory: face-to-face conversations. Engaging directly with voters, listening to their concerns, and sharing your own story fosters a personal connection that resonates deeply. As the candidate, you can lead this effort and wear out your shoes every day walking from door to door. However, to scale and reach enough people to secure a victory, you will need to build a dedicated volunteer team.

Volunteers committed to your campaign amplify your outreach efforts, allowing for more extensive voter engagement. Recruit a team to canvass neighborhoods, make phone calls, and actively listen to constituents. Volunteer canvassing, a cornerstone for getting out the vote, relies on volunteer leaders who organize and recruit teams for key voter contact events, including canvassing, phone banks, and voter registration drives.

- **Plan:** Choose a suitable location for your event, such as an office, home, business, or library. Local events in multiple locations effectively mobilize volunteers. Decide on the type of event, with canvassing being the most effective form of voter contact. However, phone banking and text banking can reach voters who might otherwise be missed. Promote your event and post it online as soon as possible to give potential volunteers multiple opportunities to get involved.

- **Recruit and retain volunteers**: Recruitment phone calls are the most effective way to ensure event success. Build a phone list of local volunteers and prospects, and call them to sign up for upcoming events. Confirm attendance through calls or texts the day before an event. Sign in volunteers to track their activity and reschedule them for future events. Remember, volunteers come for the candidate, but they stay for the community.

- **Canvass and Contact Voters**: Canvassing, or talking to voters face-to-face at their doors, is the most effective form of voter contact. Phone banking is an efficient way to persuade and mobilize voters while collecting valuable data for voter targeting. Voter registration drives are crucial for expanding your potential voter base.

- **Get out the vote:** This is the final push to persuade every undecided voter, encourage every identified supporter to make a plan to vote and reach the folks we may not have previously.

 Tip

> Here are some valuable steps for your candidate canvassing plan.

1. **Climb the ladder:** Follow the canvasser ladder of engagement to recruit digital canvassers for your campaign.

2. **Create a target list:** Develop a list of potential digital canvassers who are well-connected and likely to support your campaign. Start with the candidate and campaign staff.

3. **Organize through relationships:** Encourage friends, family, and colleagues to engage with people they know, to listen, encourage creating a plan to vote, and track contacts to confirm vote in final get out the vote.

4. **Invite and follow up with appreciation**: Invite potential canvassers using a recruitment link or through the manager canvassers platform. After inviting someone, follow up with a personal message explaining why their participation is crucial to the campaign's success.

5. **Promote volunteers to leadership roles:** After volunteers have been successful, invite them to take on leadership roles as digital organizers.

6. **Train your organizers:** Train them as an organizer or have them attend a weekly organizer training session.

7. **Make it personal:** Personal connection and follow-up are critical in this process. It is important not to overwhelm potential canvassers with too much information at once.

Target Likely Voters and Precincts

Your digital voter identification data will be very important to identify, target, and engage with your best voter segments. This strategy will help you focus your resources and phases of your campaign for maximum impact.

- **Identify voters:** Implement strategies to identify likely voters based on demographics, voting history, and issue preferences. This targeted approach ensures that campaign resources are allocated efficiently.
- **Prioritize precincts:** Prioritize key precincts by understanding their demographics and political leanings. Concentrate efforts on these areas to maximize impact and mobilize voters effectively.
- **Target and tailor your message:** Utilize data-driven microtargeting techniques to tailor your message to specific voter segments, increasing the relevance of your campaign in key precincts.

Engage Voters Across Channels

Your digital strategy is critical and your candidate website is the central hub of your election efforts. Your campaign's website serves as the primary destination for individuals to delve into the core aspects of your candidacy, providing a comprehensive resource for information, engagement, and action. The website's URL should be intuitive, memorable, and prominently featured on all campaign materials, including signage, printed materials, yard signs, and across digital and social media platforms. This ensures a seamless and direct connection for supporters, volunteers, and potential donors.

An important part of your digital strategy is to include high-quality color photos throughout campaign assets. These images should not only showcase the candidate but also convey the campaign's message and values. The visual elements play a crucial role in establishing a strong and memorable brand identity. Social media platforms, including Facebook, Instagram, Twitter, TikTok, LinkedIn, and others, serve as dynamic spaces for online conversations. The chapter underscores the significance of maintaining an active and engaging presence across these platforms, sharing not only your message but also the authentic stories of community supporters, endorsements, and the impactful work your campaign is undertaking. Importantly, video content becomes a powerful tool to humanize the candidate, share compelling narratives, and connect with voters on a personal level.

In the digital landscape, authenticity and consistency are paramount. Your message and story must resonate authentically both online and offline, creating a unified narrative that voters can easily understand and connect with. This alignment ensures that the essence of your campaign remains consistent across various channels, reinforcing the trust and connection with your audience. As a progressive political consultant, I recommend crafting a narrative that is not only compelling but also relatable, fostering a sense of community and shared values among your diverse audience.

Combine offline and online engagement with prospective voters for maximum impact. To get the attention, interest, and commitment of a prospective voter, you will likely need to reach them multiple times through different channels of engagement in-person and online. Tracking all your voter engagements through digital tools and databases is critical for your success.

- **Create your turfs:** Obtain your voter file and choose a digital tool to target your priority voters. Create canvassing

turfs using tools like Hub Builder, Hustle, OpenField, Nation Builder, NGP VAN, and others.
- **Engage in-person:** Implement traditional methods such as door-knocking, phone banking, and community outreach to engage voters personally and convey the importance of their vote with printed materials that reference your digital website and social media channels.
- **Engage with digital tools** Harness the power of digital tools and social media platforms to reach a wider audience. Develop a robust online presence, utilizing targeted ads and social media campaigns to remind and motivate voters to cast their ballots.
- **Engage across multiple channels:** Adopt a comprehensive multi-channel approach that integrates offline and online strategies to create a cohesive and impactful get-out-the-vote campaign.

★Success Story Profile: Cori Bush★

Cori Bush, a nurse, pastor, and activist, made history as the first African-American woman to represent Missouri in the U.S. House of Representatives. She serves the 1st District, which includes St. Louis and northern St. Louis County. Despite unsuccessful attempts for the U.S. Senate in 2016 and the U.S. House in 2018, she achieved victory in the 2020 U.S. House election. Featured in the 2019 Netflix film "Knock Down the House," she is now a member of the Squad in the House of Representatives.

During her 2018 campaign, Bush was described as an "insurgent" candidate and was endorsed by Brand New Congress and Justice Democrats. However, she was defeated in the Democratic primary. In 2020, she challenged incumbent Lacy Clay again and emerged victorious, a victory largely viewed as a historic upset. She received endorsements from prominent leaders such as Dr. Angela Davis, Senator Nina Turner, Congressman Ro Khanna, and Shaun King, as well as progressive organizations including Justice Democrats, Sunrise Movement, and Brand New Congress.

Bush's campaign message reflected her lived experiences and her commitment to addressing the struggles facing regular people. She focused on issues such as the impact of skyrocketing housing costs, payday lending, systemic racism in policing, and championing a Green New Deal. Her message resonated with many including support of Sunrise Movement's army of young activists, leading to her historic victory in 2020.

Her campaign received support from volunteers and progressive organizations, both in terms of campaign donations and distributed organizing efforts like texting and phone banking. These tactics allowed her campaign to reach a wide audience and effectively mobilize supporters. In her 2020 campaign, she tripled her fundraising from 2018, primarily funded by individual contributions rather than corporate donations.

Distributed Organizing to Win the Election

There are several ways to scale your voter contact and engagement to help win an election. Voter contact is most impactful through face-to-face conversations, such as knocking on doors, hosting events, and meeting people while tabling at farmers' markets and other community locations.

- **Canvass with digital tools:** These tools can also be powerful for engaging with people through texting, instant messaging, videos, and conversations on social media.
- **Host a postcard party:** Recruit volunteers to write and send

postcards. These postcards can contain personal stories about why the volunteer supports the candidate and the important issues in the campaign. Be sure to plan to order postcards with a color photo image of the candidate, key message, and contact information for learning more and getting involved. Time the delivery of the postcards to coincide with early voting and the final day of the election. This ensures that your message is fresh in voters' minds when they cast their ballots.

- **Write letters to the editor:** Writing letters to the editor is a powerful way to support your candidate, campaign, or cause.

 Tip

Letters to the editor are free and provide a direct personal voice from a person who supports your, campaign, candidate or cause to other people interested in learning more. Here are some tips to guide you:

1. **Choose your topic:** The letter can be written to address a specific issue highlighted in the local newspaper, to raise awareness for a candidate or cause, or to share a personal story to spark interest and engagement.

2. **Submit your letter:** Typically, these letters are published in the Opinion section and can be submitted online or via traditional mail. The letters that are most relevant to the audience and interesting to readers will be most likely to be published.

3. **Engage with readers:** After publishing, there will often be online comments to generate discussions. It can be helpful to track these discussions and post URL links to additional resources and information to help educate and encourage analysis.

4. **Amplify your message:** Be sure to amplify your letter via social media channels including Facebook and Twitter to further expand the reach.

5. **Write your story:** Write your story about your issue or candidate that reflects your personal experience or story. How is it relevant to your community or neighborhood? What are the values that are being discussed that inspired you to action? What other stories exist in the community that will compel interest, discussion, and engagement?

Plan for Final Week of Election

In the final weekend before the election, your final drive to get out the vote is critical. Up to 50% of voters may not vote until election day, so it is crucial to have all your volunteers lined up for important roles. Your strategy should be targeted and your positioning should be based on the momentum you have built going into the final weekend.

This strategy will include election day and beyond. Plan for post-election monitoring to make sure all votes are counted and any problems are sorted out. Since many votes aren't counted on election day due to mail-in and provisional ballots, this process can take days or even weeks.

After the election, carry out a review to assess the campaign's strengths and weaknesses. Share this information with volunteers and supporting organizations as best practices. Whether you win or lose, there are many things you must do to wrap up your campaign. This includes taking down lawn signs, paying bills, finishing reports for the state, closing out bank accounts, and reassembling your house.

 **Tip**

During the final weeks, you will be extremely busy to get out the vote so it is important to plan and prepare a schedule of important activities before, during, and after the election.

1. **Appreciate your team:** Make sure to show gratitude to all your volunteers and voters. They are the heart of any successful campaign. Their hard work and dedication deserve recognition. You could send personalized thank-you notes or emails, host a volunteer appreciation event, or start a social media campaign to spotlight your volunteers and supporters' contributions.

2. **Get out the vote and celebrate:** During the final days it is critical to have all your people available to encourage voters to cast their ballots. As the candidate, be ready to deliver an inspiring speech to your volunteers and voters, regardless of the election outcome.

3. **Count every vote:** Set up a team to watch the vote counting to ensure all votes are counted correctly on

election day and the days after. Vote counting is a key part of any election, and it is important to have a team ready to ensure all votes are counted accurately and efficiently. Make sure your team is well-trained and has the resources they need to do their job effectively. Plan for the next few days as more ballots will be counted. In many elections, more ballots are counted in the days after the election. It is important to have a plan to monitor the vote count and address any issues that come up. Have a team in place to monitor the vote count and provide regular updates to your campaign staff and supporters.

4. **Communicate appreciation:** Plan to send emails the day of the election and the day after to encourage voter turnout, appreciate your volunteers and voters and continue to lead your message to sustain the movement.

5. **Renew, rest, restore:** After the election, it's important to reflect and learn. Schedule a review process with your team and volunteer leaders. Discuss what worked, what didn't, and how you can improve. This will help you maintain momentum and build power over time.

Chapter Checklist: Get Out the Vote

In the spirit of Susan B. Anthony, who once said, "Someone struggled for your right to vote. Use it," this chapter delved into the crucial step of getting out the vote. Running a political campaign is an exciting adventure that requires hard work, commitment, and a clear understanding of your goals and values. Win or lose, this experience will leave a lasting impact on you and your community. In the next chapter, you will take steps to ensure all votes are counted, review your campaign's outcome, and acknowledge all your supporters who volunteered and voted. Here is your chapter checklist.

✓ **Checklist:**

1. You developed a successful plan to encourage voter turnout, learning about its key elements.
2. You organized effective voter registration drives to maximize election turnout.
3. You utilized various channels to remind people to vote and learned how to use them effectively.
4. You ensured your message reached your targeted voters through strategic planning.
5. You learned how to redirect negative campaigning from opponents and used it as an opportunity to restate your message.
6. Your work ethic and values impacted the success of your campaign and inspired others to work hard for you.
7. You practiced humility and active listening, understanding their importance in a political campaign.
8. You kept a smile on your face and enjoyed the campaign process, staying positive no matter what happened.

Nine

Count Every Vote

Success is peace of mind which is a direct result of self-satisfaction in knowing you did your best to become the best you are capable of.

—*John Wooden*

John Wooden, a coach and teacher, is widely regarded as the greatest NCAA basketball head coach of all time winning ten NCAA national basketball championships. However, his greatest accomplishments were not limited to basketball. He united a community, inspired them with victories, and showed them how to turn dreams into reality through mastering basic skills.

Born in 1910, his journey started on a humble farm where he learned the importance of hard work and discipline from his father. These early lessons laid the foundation for what would later become his renowned Pyramid of Success, a roadmap for individual and team excellence, life principles, and a roadmap to being a better person.

Coach began his career with a modest 6-11 record in his first year, marking his only losing season. As a teacher and coach, he emphasized the importance of the journey. He believed in building success step by step through sustained effort, continuous learning, and self-improvement. In 1948, Wooden became the head basketball coach at UCLA. Despite less-than-ideal facilities, he instilled discipline in his team, turning them into strong competitors. Their hard work led to four perfect 30-0 seasons, 10 national championships, and an impressive 664-162 record under Wooden's leadership. He was honored as NCAA College Basketball Coach of the Year six times and made history by being the first person to be inducted into the Naismith Memorial Basketball Hall of Fame as both a player and a coach.

Wooden's teachings extend beyond sports, emphasizing the joy of the journey and the satisfaction of knowing you have done your best, regardless of the outcome. This chapter, inspired by his philosophy, underscores the importance of continuous learning and building a foundation for success. You have worked diligently on the steps in this book to support your campaign, candidate, and cause. In this final chapter, you will learn crucial steps to take after the election.

- **Appreciate:** Thank your volunteers, supporters, and donors for their dedication at your election night gathering.
- **Count every vote:** Keep an eye on the post-election process to make sure every vote is counted fairly and transparently.
- **Wrap up your campaign:** Remove signs, pay bills, file reports, close accounts, and tidy up your campaign office.
- **Review your goals and outcomes:** Evaluate your results including strengths and weaknesses and share your feedback and best practices with other progressive campaigns and organizations.
- **Learn and never give up:** Learn from successful campaigns that continued to run for office, support candidates, and serve their communities.

- **Rest, restore, and renew:** Take time to rest and rejuvenate after the campaign, preparing yourself to face new challenges.

During the final days of your campaign, it will feel like a rollercoaster ride—both challenging and exhilarating. As you prepare for Election Day and the culmination of all your hard work, it is essential to gear up for the post-election steps. Most likely, you will be exhausted, emotional, and facing some unknowns, so be sure to plan.

Whether you win or lose, you need to prepare to appreciate your supporters, shut down your campaign, and gather important metrics for your assessment process. It is very important to take care of yourself and your supporters on election day with proper self-care, including eating, staying hydrated, and planning for a potential late-night speech. After the election, support your team in monitoring the final vote process, collecting feedback, and planning the next steps, emphasizing the importance of rest, restoration, and renewal for the journey ahead.

Appreciate Your Supporters

Thank your volunteers, supporters, and donors for their dedication, and invite them to an election night gathering. A successful campaign is not just about winning the election, but the peace of mind that comes from knowing you and all your supporters have done your best. This is the essence of a successful campaign - striving for personal and collective growth, and knowing that you have given your all, regardless of the outcome.

Now imagine it is election night and you just delivered your speech, thanking your volunteers, your campaign team, and your supporters. You have put in months of hard work, attending events, motivating volunteers, and meeting voters face-to-face. You are tired, but the job is not over. In many ways, your journey is just beginning. The days and weeks following the election are critical for your campaign, particularly if the race is tight.

 Tip

Thank your volunteers, supporters, and donors for their dedication. This not only acknowledges their hard work but also fosters a sense of community and shared achievement.

1. **Express your gratitude:** Always express your gratitude to your supporters. Their hard work and dedication have contributed significantly to your campaign.

2. **Recognize the hard work:** Acknowledge the efforts of your volunteers and donors. Recognition can be a powerful motivator and can help strengthen their commitment to your cause.

3. **Communicate the next steps:** Keep your supporters informed about the progress of your campaign. Regular updates can help them feel more involved and invested in your cause.

4. **Celebrate:** Organize an election night gathering to celebrate the efforts of your team. This can be a great way to thank your supporters and reflect on the campaign.

5. **Continue engagement:** Even after the campaign, keep

> in touch with your supporters. Their continued involvement can be invaluable for future campaigns or causes

Count Every Vote

It is critical to ensure every vote is counted fairly and transparently. Keep an eye on the post-election process for any issues or irregularities that could affect the outcome. Be ready for any legal challenges or recounts that might come up. Communicate with the media, the public, and authorities about the election status and results.

Ensuring every vote is counted fairly and transparently is a crucial part of a democratic election. U.S. elections are decentralized, with each state setting its laws and shaping the roles counties play leading up to Election Day. At the federal level, the president is elected indirectly through an Electoral College, while Congress members are directly elected by the people of each state. There are also many elected offices at the state level, including at least a governor and legislature. Local-level elections occur in counties, cities, towns, townships, boroughs, and villages.

Elections are typically managed by county or municipal officials, with state and federal governments also playing roles. The official in charge of elections can vary by state and maybe a county auditor, clerk, or commissioner of elections. They oversee voting machine allocation, and polling location management, and ensure the polling process is accessible, secure, and efficient.

Volunteers, or poll workers, are crucial to running elections. They open the polls, check in voters, issue ballots, assist voters, implement election laws and procedures, maintain the chain of custody of ballots and voting equipment, close the polls, and reconcile the number of voters with the number of ballots cast.

This complex process is fundamental to the functioning of democracy in the United States, ensuring that the will of the people is accurately represented in government. It requires the coordinated efforts of numerous individuals and organizations at various levels, all working together to uphold the principles of fairness, transparency, and inclusivity.

Election monitoring, the process of observing and assessing the conduct of an election, helps protect the integrity and legitimacy of the election and identifies and addresses any issues or irregularities that may affect the outcome.

- **Monitor before the election:** Observing the legal framework, electoral administration, voter registration, candidate nomination, campaign environment, media coverage, voter education, and security situation before the election.

- **Monitor the day of the election:** Observing the opening, voting, closing, and counting processes at polling stations, and assessing voter turnout, ballot secrecy, polling station accessibility, procedure compliance, polling staff performance, presence of party agents or other observers, and any incidents or complaints.

- **Monitor after the election:** Observe the tabulation, transmission, aggregation, and announcement of results, assess the accuracy, transparency, and timeliness of the process, and handle any appeals or disputes.

Election monitoring can provide valuable information and recommendations to improve the quality and credibility of the election and enhance public confidence and trust in the process.

Wrap Up Your Campaign

Whether you win or lose, it is important to conclude your campaign gracefully. Handle practical matters like removing signs, paying bills, filing reports, closing accounts, and closing your campaign office. Acknowledge your opponent and either congratulate them on their effort and victory or offer your support and cooperation. Avoid blaming or criticizing anyone for a loss gloating or boasting about a win.

Most importantly, you need to learn from your experience and improve your future campaigns. You need to conduct a post-election evaluation of your campaign's strengths and weaknesses and share your feedback and best practices with your team and other progressive campaigns and organizations. You need to celebrate your achievements and improvements and identify your opportunities and challenges. You need to reflect on your goals and values and renew your commitment and passion.

Review Goals and Outcomes

Evaluate the strengths and weaknesses and share your feedback and best practices with other progressive campaigns and organizations.

Collect all relevant data and feedback about the campaign. Analyze the data to identify trends, strengths, and weaknesses. Discuss the findings with the campaign team and any external observers. Document the findings in the campaign evaluation template. Review the completed evaluation and reflect on the lessons learned.

Encourage an open and honest discussion about the campaign's successes and failures. Emphasize that the purpose of the evaluation is to learn and improve, not to assign blame. Take time to celebrate the campaign's successes, no matter how small. Acknowledge the challenges faced during the campaign and discuss how they can be addressed in the future. Use the evaluation as a tool for planning future campaigns.

Campaign Evaluation Template

- **Candidate, office, campaign team:** Basic information about the candidate, the office they're running for, and the campaign team.
- **Election results:** Detailed results of the election, including the percentage of votes received by the candidate.
- **Turnout:** Information about voter turnout, including any notable demographic trends.
- **Campaign goals and overview:** A summary of the campaign, including its goals, and key events.
- **Campaign strengths, weaknesses, opportunities, and threats (SWOT):** Detailed analysis of what worked well and what did not work well in the campaign.
- **Campaign theme and issues:** Information about the campaign's main message and the key issues it focused on.
- **Campaign coordination:** Details about how the campaign was coordinated, including any partnerships with other organizations.
- **Campaign leadership:** Information about the campaign's leadership structure.
- **Fundraising:** Details about the campaign's fundraising efforts.

City Council Candidate Evaluation

Navigating the city council race amid a crowded field of eight candidates proved to be a formidable task, and our candidate faced the uphill challenge of competing against seasoned contenders with established political backgrounds.

- **Candidate, office, and campaign team**: Our candidate, a newcomer to the political scene, faced the formidable task of navigating a city council race amid a crowded field of eight candidates. The campaign team, though small, showcased exceptional dedication and effectiveness.

- **Election results**: Despite the uphill challenge of competing against seasoned contenders with established political backgrounds, our candidate demonstrated remarkable resilience, securing a significant number of votes in a closely contested battle for the four available offices.

- **Turnout**: The election saw a robust turnout, with voters valuing experience, as evident in the successful bids of the incumbent council members, former mayor, and planning commission members.

- **Campaign goals and overview**: The campaign aimed to bring fresh perspectives to the city council, with a particular focus on affordable housing. Despite entering the race at the eleventh hour and facing initial shortcomings due to limited planning time, the campaign made a significant impact.

- **SWOT analysis**: Strengths of the campaign included the candidate's public speaking skills and clear, compelling message. Weaknesses included limited name recognition and resources. Opportunities existed in the candidate's unique positioning as the sole advocate for affordable housing. Threats included the crowded field and the voters' preference for experienced candidates.

- **Campaign theme and issues**: The campaign centered on the pivotal issue of affordable housing, which resonated strongly with the community. The successful passage of the affordable housing measure marked a significant triumph.

- **Campaign coordination**: The campaign was coordinated by a dedicated team of volunteer leaders, who worked tirelessly despite resource constraints.

- **Campaign leadership**: Our candidate led the campaign, leveraging a background in public speaking to excel in debates and forums.

- **Fundraising**: The campaign operated on a limited budget, underscoring the critical importance of meticulous planning and strategic foresight in future political endeavors.

Despite falling short of victory, the campaign served as a valuable learning experience. The limited budget and time constraints underscored the critical importance of meticulous planning and strategic foresight in future political endeavors.

Turn a Setback into Success

Running a campaign is a challenging but rewarding journey that can teach you a lot about yourself and the democratic process. Each loss is as valuable as each win when you continuously learn and grow. Every single vote does matter, so count every vote and celebrate your achievements.

Setbacks are an inevitable part of life, and they can be discouraging. However, setbacks can also be opportunities for growth and learning. In this section, you will explore strategies, success stories from progressive campaigns, candidates, and causes, and tips on how to turn setbacks into successes.

An important lesson for running a successful campaign is to encourage a culture of ongoing learning and feedback among your team, volunteers, and supporters. This approach can help enhance skills, knowledge, and performance, and identify and address any gaps, challenges, or opportunities in your campaign.

 Tip

Explore these strategies for continuous learning.

1. **Foster a growth mindset:** Establish clear, achievable goals for yourself and your team, and monitor your progress. Offer timely, constructive feedback to improve performance. Treat successes and failures as learning opportunities. Learn from the experiences and perspectives of mentors, peers, experts, or supporters. Maintain an optimistic attitude and avoid negative self-talk or criticism.

2. **Provide learning resources:** Compile relevant learning resources for your team and update them regularly. Resources can include books, articles, podcasts, videos, courses, webinars, workshops, or online platforms. Motivate your team to use resources that suit their needs and interests. Offer support on how to use resources

effectively and apply them to campaign goals. Ask for suggestions on the quality and usefulness of resources, and make improvements as needed.

3. **Personalize learning paths:** Help create personalized learning plans for roles and goals. Offer feedback and help overcome obstacles in the learning process. Evaluate learning progress and celebrate achievements. Promote the sharing of learning plans and experiences., Make time for learning: Schedule time on your calendar for individual and group learning spaces. Set reminders or alarms for your learning time slots. Balance your learning time with other tasks. Reflect on your learning time and adjust it as needed.

4. **Promote knowledge sharing:** Create a platform for knowledge sharing and collaboration. Promote working together to achieve common goals. Encourage a growth mindset and the belief that you can develop your abilities and potential through effort, practice, and feedback.

5. **Celebrate learning milestones:** Define and track learning milestones. Reward yourself and others upon reaching milestones. Share your learning journey and thank supporters. Reflect on progress, strengths, areas for improvement, and encountered hurdles and opportunities.

Never Give Up the Fight

Win or lose, you can learn from successful campaigns, candidates, and causes that inspire with stories of reliance, dedication, and never giving up and continuing to serve their communities.

Persistence pays off for candidates who run until elected to overcome electoral defeats and achieve victory. Politics is not easy. It demands bravery, strong beliefs, and dedication to your vision, even when faced with opposition or failure. Many politicians have experienced defeat, but some have used these setbacks as learning opportunities, refining their strategies, and rallying their supporters for future success. There are many examples of progressive campaigns, candidates, and causes that have faced setbacks but continue to fight.

These examples serve as a testament to the power of resilience and the impact of never giving up the fight, no matter the obstacles faced. They inspire us to continue serving our communities and fighting for what we believe in.

- **Women's right to vote**: The fight for women's right to vote was a long and arduous one. Despite facing numerous setbacks, suffragists never gave up. Their resilience eventually led to the passage of the 19th Amendment in 1920, granting women the right to vote.
- **Civil rights**: Despite facing severe opposition and violence, civil rights activists continued their fight for equality. Leaders like Martin Luther King Jr. and Rosa Parks faced numerous setbacks but never gave up. Their resilience led to landmark legislation like the Civil Rights Act of 1964 and the Voting Rights Act of 1965.
- **Labor rights**: The labor movement in the United States grew out of the need to protect the common interest of workers. Despite facing numerous setbacks, labor unions fought for better wages, reasonable hours, and safer working conditions.

Their resilience led to landmark legislation like the Civil Rights Act of 1964 and the Voting Rights Act of 1965.

- **Marriage equality:** The battle for marriage equality was a tough, decades-long journey. Despite numerous challenges, LGBTQ activists and allies achieved a landmark victory in 2015 with the nationwide legalization of same-sex marriage. Their unwavering commitment to justice and equality was key to their success.
- **Environmental justice:** The fight for environmental justice has been an ongoing struggle for decades. The Sunrise Movement, a youth-led group, is advocating for climate justice and a Green New Deal. Despite resistance from powerful fossil fuel interests and slow political action on climate change, they've built a strong grassroots movement demanding bold climate action. Their success is largely due to their ability to mobilize youth and build a diverse coalition committed to a just and sustainable future.

Many politicians ran for office multiple times before achieving victory.

- **Barbara Lee**, a U.S. representative from California since 1998, is known for her progressive views and criticism of the Iraq War. However, her political journey wasn't easy. In 1990, she lost her bid for city attorney in Oakland, California. Undeterred, she ran for the California State Assembly the same year and won. She served in the state assembly until 1996, then in the state senate until 1998. That year, she ran for the U.S. House of Representatives to succeed her mentor, Ron Dellums, and won by a narrow margin, becoming the

first African-American woman to represent the Bay Area in Congress.
- **Cori Bush**, a U.S. representative from Missouri since 2021, is a member of The Squad and co-chair of the Congressional Cannabis Caucus. Her political journey began in 2016 when she ran for the U.S. Senate in Missouri but lost in the Democratic primary. In 2018, she challenged incumbent Lacy Clay for a seat in the U.S. House of Representatives but was defeated. Undeterred, she ran again in 2020 with increased support and managed to unseat Clay, ending his family's long hold on the seat, and becoming the first African-American woman to represent Missouri in Congress.
- **Stacey Abrams** is a political leader, voting rights activist, and author. She served as the minority leader of the Georgia House of Representatives from 2011 to 2017, making history as the first Black woman to lead in the state legislature. In 2018, she was the first Black woman to be a major party's nominee for governor. Despite narrowly losing the election amid voter suppression allegations, she launched a campaign to expose Georgia's electoral system flaws. Abrams' efforts in mobilizing and registering voters, particularly in the Black community, were instrumental in the Democrats' significant wins in Georgia in 2020.
- **Pamela Price,** a civil rights attorney, and political activist has been the district attorney of Alameda County, California since 2022. Her first run for public office was in 2018, challenging incumbent district attorney Nancy O'Malley, but she lost. In 2020, she ran for mayor of Oakland, California, but came in fourth place. In 2022, she ran again for district attorney of Alameda County and won, becoming the first Black woman to hold this position.

- **Jamaal Bowman** ran for the New York State Senate in 2016 but lost in the primary. He attempted to run again in 2018 but withdrew from the race. In 2020, he ran for Congress in New York's 16th district and defeated the 16-term incumbent Eliot Engel in the primary. He became a rising star of the progressive and socialist movement and a member of The Squad. He emerged as a prominent figure in the progressive movement and joined The Squad.
- **Bernie Sanders'** political path, marked by initial setbacks, saw him run as a third-party candidate for various offices before narrowly winning the Burlington mayoral race in 1981 by just 10 votes. He served four terms as mayor, then advanced to the U.S. House of Representatives and the Senate. Sanders, known for his commitment to social justice, economic equality, and environmental sustainability, has cultivated a robust grassroots movement that continues to inspire millions.

These progressive leaders show that with determination, resilience, and a clear vision, setbacks can be turned into comebacks. Progressive ideas and values resonate with voters, and progressive change is possible. They have inspired many others to follow in their footsteps, challenge the status quo, make history, and continue to make a difference.

 Tip

Failures, rejection, and losses are valuable and important to achieve success in life and progressive campaigns, candidates, and causes. Stay strong, resilience and recognize that loss, rejection, and setbacks are inevitable in both your personal and progressive life, but can be overcome with preparation, persistence, and learning.

1. **Reframe failure**: View failure as a source of motivation and improvement, not discouragement and defeat. Keep trying until you succeed.

2. **Believe in your cause**: Let your belief and confidence in your campaign, candidate, or cause be your driving force. Don't give up if you have something valuable and unique to offer.

3. **Embrace setbacks**: Turn your setbacks into successes. See failure as an opportunity for growth and learning.

4. **Take risks**: Don't be afraid to try new things and step out of your comfort zone.

5. **Build a support network**: Surround yourself with a supportive network of friends, family, and colleagues.

6. **Stay focused**: Keep your eyes on your goals. Don't let obstacles deter you.

7. **Persist**: Persistence is key. Don't give up, even when things seem tough.

8. **Celebrate Victories**: Celebrate every victory, big or small. Use them to fuel your journey. Setbacks are stepping stones to success and opportunities for growth.

★Success Story Profile: Kareem Abdul-Jabbar★

Kareem Abdul-Jabbar, a basketball legend, has seamlessly transitioned from the courts to a prolific career as a writer, leader, and social justice advocate. His commitment to excellence, integrity, and inspiring others is well-known. His success began at UCLA under coach John Wooden, whose teachings he carried throughout his career and life.

You undoubtedly recognize Kareem Abdul-Jabbar as the NBA legend who dominated the courts with his signature Skyhook, winning six championships and earning numerous MVP titles. Yet, Abdul-Jabbar's impact extends far beyond the basketball arena. Since hanging up his jersey, he's wielded the power of the written word to champion progressive causes and amplify voices often overlooked in American history.

Abdul-Jabbar's transition from basketball icon to influential writer and advocate for social justice is nothing short of inspiring. His literary contributions include works like "Black Profiles in Courage" and "On the Shoulders of Giants," shedding light on the achievements and struggles of People of Color in American history. As a cultural ambassador and recipient of the Presidential Medal of Freedom, Abdul-Jabbar has utilized his public voice to address social injustice and fight for what's right.

In a memorable speech at the 2016 Democratic National Convention, Abdul-Jabbar didn't shy away from addressing political issues. Criticizing Donald Trump's divisive views on Muslims, he passionately declared, "*Donald Trump's idea to register Muslims and prevent them from entering our country is the very tyranny Thomas Jefferson abhorred.*" This bold stance showcased Abdul-Jabbar's commitment to using his celebrity status to advocate for progressive issues and rights. Now, on Substack, he continues to explore the intersection of sports, politics, and popular culture, sharing his insights on topics ranging from basketball championships to protests against laws restricting marginalized rights. Kareem Abdul-Jabbar's journey from the courts to the keyboard exemplifies the transformative power of using one's influence for meaningful change.

Despite his successes, Abdul-Jabbar has faced challenges. He's been a vocal advocate for social justice, speaking out against racism and inequality. In 2020, he was diagnosed with a rare form of leukemia, which he has since overcome. His resilience in the face of adversity and his advocacy work continue to inspire others in the fight for equality and justice.

Rest, Renew, and Restore

Sustaining resilience is an ongoing process. You need to be prepared for the unexpected and be able to adapt in the middle of the political storm. While campaigns, candidates, and causes often rely on routines, these may not be necessary in times of change, uncertainty, or crisis. It is important to rest, renew, and restore to sustain yourself and your team.

Flexibility is key. Be ready to adapt and add improvisations to your toolkit. This involves analyzing your tools, questioning routine assumptions, and letting go. By incorporating these strategies, you can build resilience, helping you to thrive even in the face of uncertainty and change.

After the campaign, take time to rejuvenate yourself and prepare for new challenges. Sustaining your energy and effectiveness in your community, campaign, or cause is vital. Remember, resilience is not just about weathering the storm, but also about taking the time to rest, renew, and restore. This balance is key to the long-term success of any campaign, candidate, or cause.

- **Prevent burnout:** Avoid continuous work without rest to prevent burnout and maintain productivity and enthusiasm.
- **Improve health**: Regular rest and renewal can improve your physical and mental health, boosting your resilience.
- **Boost creativity**: Rest can enhance your creativity and problem-solving skills, leading to innovative solutions.
- **Focus your energy:** Rest and renewal can enhance your focus and attention, making you more effective in your tasks.
- **Sustain your work:** By taking care of yourself, you ensure that you can continue to contribute to your cause over the long term.

 Tip

> Here are some ideas to sustain your energy, rejuvenate your spirit, and renew your health:
>
> 1. **Take regular breaks:** Do not wait until you're exhausted to take a break. Schedule regular breaks throughout your day to rest and rejuvenate.
>
> 2. **Walk outdoors:** Get some exercise and fresh air to walk in nature.
>
> 3. **Practice self-care:** Engage in activities that you enjoy and that help you relax. This could be reading, exercising, meditating, or spending time in nature.
>
> 4. **Stay hydrated and eat healthy:** Your physical health

directly impacts your energy levels. Make sure to stay hydrated and eat a balanced diet.

5. **Get enough sleep:** Ensure you're getting enough sleep each night. Good sleep is essential for rest and renewal.

6. **Connect with others:** Spend time with friends, family, or colleagues who uplift and support you. Social connections can provide emotional support and help you unwind.

In this pivotal moment in history, there are significant challenges in our communities, country, and the world. These include the climate crisis, unprecedented income and wealth inequality, pandemics, a lack of trust in our systems and government, the emergence of artificial intelligence, a fragmented healthcare system, gun violence, and the rise of right-wing extremism, conflicts, and division. These challenges can seem overwhelming, but change is possible, and you are powerful.

Despite the magnitude of the challenges we face, there are countless stories of optimism and people power. A rising generation that is more diverse, equitable, and inclusive is stepping up to make a difference. Workers and unions are fighting back, and more people are recognizing the need for change. These stories highlight the resilience and determination of individuals and communities. They are reminders that you have the power to create change every day.

As you navigate these challenges and work towards a better future, it is very important to take time to rest, renew, and restore. Sustainable change requires sustainable activists. As you fight for your campaign, candidate, or cause, be sure to take care of yourself and support those around you. The road ahead may be long and difficult, but together, we can make a difference. The extraordinary challenges we face are very real, but you have the power to create change every day. Let's harness that power and move forward together.

Chapter Checklist: Count Every Vote

Inspired by the teachings of John Wooden, this chapter emphasizes the joy of the journey and the satisfaction of knowing you have done your best, regardless of the outcome. It underscores the importance of continuous learning and building a foundation for success. As you have worked diligently on the steps in this book to support your campaign, candidate, or cause, this final chapter provides crucial steps to take after the election.

The journey does not end with the election. The lessons learned, the connections made, and the changes initiated continue to ripple out, influencing your community and beyond. Keep moving forward, keep learning, and keep striving for success. Your journey continues.

✓ **Checklist:**

1. You showed appreciation by thanking your volunteers, supporters, and donors for their dedication and inviting them to an election night gathering.
2. You ensured every vote counts by keeping an eye on the post-election process to make sure every vote was counted fairly and transparently.
3. You wrapped up your campaign by removing signs, paying bills, filing reports, closing accounts, and tidying up your campaign office.
4. You assessed your campaign by evaluating its strengths and weaknesses and shared your feedback and best practices with other progressive campaigns and organizations.
5. You were inspired by success stories and learned from successful campaigns that continued to run for office, support candidates, and serve their communities.
6. You took time to rest, restore, and renew after the campaign, preparing yourself to face new challenges.

Resources

Step 1: READY

1. "John Lennon." https://www.johnlennon.com.
2. "Imagine Peace." https://www.imaginepeace.com.

Chapter One: Find Your Purpose

1. "Sanders, Bernie." *Our Revolution: A Future to Believe In*. NY: St Martin's Press, 2016.
2. "Sanders, Bernie and John Nichols." *It's OK to Be Angry about Capitalism*. NY: Crown Publishing Group, 2023.
3. "Lao Tzu." https://www.famousphilosophers.org/lao-tzu.
4. "Miralles, Francesc, and Hector Garcia." *Ikigai: The Japanese Secret to a Long and Happy Life*. NY: Penguin Books, 2016.
5. "Cat & Dog First Aid Online Training." Red Cross. https://www.redcross.org/take-a-class/first-aid/cat-dog-first-aid.
6. "Trusted Housesitters." https://www.trustedhousesitters.com.
7. "Danny Glover." http://www.mrdannyglover.com.
8. "Greta Thunberg." Britannica. https://www.britannica.com/biography/Greta-Thunberg.
9. "Jackie Robinson." https://jackierobinson.com.
10. "President James Carter." The White House. https://www.whitehouse.gov/about-the-white-house/presidents/james-carter.
11. "The Carter Center. Waging Peace. Fighting Disease. Building Hope." https://www.cartercenter.org/about/experts/jimmy_carter.html.
12. "Carter Work Project with Habitat for Humanity." Habitat for Humanity. https://www.habitat.org/carter-work-project.

Chapter Two: Get Involved

1. "Muhammad Ali." Britannica. https://www.britannica.com/biography/Muhammad-Ali-boxer.
2. "AARP." https://aarp.org/volunteer.
3. "Dr. Ethel Percy Andrus." AARP. https://www.aarp.org/about-aarp/history/ethel-percy-andrus-biography.html.
4. "Volunteer Match." https://www.volunteermatch.org.
5. "AmeriCorps." https://americorps.gov.
6. "Margaret Mead." https://www.britannica.com/biography/Margaret-Mead.
7. "American Society for the Prevention of Cruelty to Animals." https://www.aspca.org.
8. "Best Friends." https://bestfriends.org.
9. "The Humane Society." https://www.humanesociety.org.
10. "MexiPetsMexipets Animal Rescue." https://www.mexipetsanimalrescue.org.
11. "Association of Gleaning Organizations." https://gleaningorgs.com.
12. "Bethlehem House of Bread." https://bethlehemhouseofbread.org.
13. "Oregon Food Bank." https://www.oregonfoodbank.org.
14. "Portland Fruit Tree Project."https://www.portlandfruit.org.
15. "American Civil Liberties Union."https://www.aclu.org.
16. "Black Youth Project." https://blackyouthproject.com.
17. "Las Americas Immigrant Advocacy Center." https://www.lasamericas.org.
18. "National Association for the Advancement of Colored People." https://naacp.org.
19. "Southern Poverty Law Center." https://www.splcenter.org.
20. "Democratic Socialists of America." https://www.dsausa.org.
21. "Indivisible." https://indivisible.org.
22. "Our Revolution." https://ourrevolution.com/ourstory.
23. "Our Revolution East Bay." https://www.facebook.com/OurRevolution-EastBay.
24. "350.org." https://350.org.
25. "Food & Water Watch." https://www.foodandwaterwatch.org.
26. "Greenpeace." https://www.greenpeace.org/global.
27. "Sierra Club."https://www.sierraclub.org.
28. "Subject to Climate."https://subjecttoclimate.org.
29. "Sunrise Movement."https://www.sunrisemovement.org.

Resources

30. "Brady United." https://www.bradyunited.org.
31. "Everytown for Gun Safety." https://www.everytown.org.
32. "Giffords.Courage to Fight Gun Violence." https://giffords.org.
33. "March for Our Lives." https://marchforourlives.com.
34. "Moms Demand Action." https://momsdemandaction.org.
35. "Sandy Hook Promise." https://www.sandyhookpromise.org.
36. "Students Demand Action." https://studentsdemandaction.org.
37. "Commoncause.org." https://www.commoncause.org.
38. "Headcount." https://www.headcount.org.
39. "Independent Voter Project." https://independentvoterproject.org.
40. "League of Women Voters." https://www.lwv.org.
41. "Rock the Vote." https://www.rockthevote.org.
42. "When We All Vote." https://whenweallvote.org.
43. "Cityside Journalism." https://citysidejournalism.org.
44. "Berkelyside." https://www.berkeleyside.org.
45. "Oaklandside." https://oaklandside.org.
46. "Richmondside." https://richmondside.org.
47. "California Writers Club." https://calwriters.org.
48. "Foundation for Individual Rights and Expression." https://www.thefire.org.
49. "National Writers Union." https://nwu.org.
50. "Willamette Writers." https://willamettewriters.org.
51. "The Muhammad Ali Center." https://alicenter.org.
52. "Athletes for Hope." https://www.athletesforhope.org.
53. "Big Brothers Big Sisters of America." https://www.bbbs.org.
54. "Special Olympics." https://www.specialolympics.org.
55. "Girls on the Run." https://www.girlsontherun.org.
56. "The First Tee." https://firsttee.org.
57. "Diveheart Foundation." https://www.diveheart.org.
58. "Sierra Club Local Outings." https://www.sierraclub.org/local-outdoors.
59. "Arena." https://www.arena.run.
60. "Run for Something." https://runforsomething.net.

Chapter 3: Create Your Plan

1. "Franklin, Ben." *America's Original Entrepreneur. Franklin's Autobiography for Modern Times.* Adapted by Blaine McCormick. Canada: Eliot House Productions, 2005.

2. "Ben Franklin." University of Pennsylvania Archives. https://archives.upenn.edu/exhibits/penn-people/biography/benjamin-franklin/.
3. "Smith, Sharon J." *The Young Activists Guide to Building a Green Movement + Changing the World.* Berkeley: Ten Speed Press, 2011.
4. "Hawkes, Suzanne.""Purpose, Outcome, Plan (POP) Process." suzannehawkes.com/2010/04/09/pop-everything.
5. "Assembly Delegate Selections." California Democratic Party. cadem.org/wp-content/uploads/2020/06/2019-ADEMs-QUICK-REFERENCE-Administrative-Deadline-5.pdf.
6. "Habitat for Humanity." Habitat.org.

Step 2: SET

1. "Bill McKibben." https://billmckibben.com.
2. "Third Act." https://thirdact.org.

Chapter 4: Form Your Organization

1. *Politics the Wellstone Way. How to Elect Progressive Candidates and Win on Issues.* Minneapolis: Weststone Action, University of Minnesota Press, 2005.
2. "California Democratic Council: Starting a New Democratic Club". https://caldc.org.
3. "Indivisible: A Practical Guide to Resisting the Trump Agenda". Originally published on December 11, 2016. https://indivisible.org/resource/organize-local-group-fight-your-congressional-district.
4. "National Equity Project." https://www.nationalequityproject.org.
5. "Our Revolution East Bay: Bylaws." https://www.facebook.com/OurRevolutionEastBay.
6. "SF Berniecrats: How to Start Your Own Local Group." https://sfberniecrats.com/how-to-start-your-own-local-group/.
7. "How to Start a Nonprofit That Doesn't Fail." bossonabudget.com.

Chapter 5: Run for Office

1. "Shirley Chisolm, First African American woman to be elected to the

U.S. Congress." Britannica. https://britannica.com/biography/Shirley-Chisholm.
2. "How Many Politicians Are There in the US?" Poliengine. https://poliengine.com/blog/how-many-politicians-are-there-in-the-us.
3. "Run for Office." https://runforoffice.org.
4. "The U.S. and About the U.S. and Its Government." https://www.usa.gov/about-the-us.
5. "LDF Thurgood Marshall Institute. Guide to Local Elections." Thurgood Marshall Institute. https://tminstituteldf.org/local-elections.
6. McMullen, Catherine. "Clackamas County Clerk."https://clackamasvoice.org.
7. Ehrlich, April. "Clackamas County voters elect new clerk following major ballot gaffes." OPB. Nov. 9, 2022. https://www.opb.org/article/2022/11/09/clackamas-county-clerk-election-oregon-sherry-hall-catherine-mcmullen.
8. "National District Attorneys Association. What is a DA?" National District Attorneys Association. https://ndaa.org/about/what-does-a-da-do.
9. Price, Pamela. "Alameda County District Attorney." https://www.pamelaprice4da.com.
10. "Congresswoman Barbara Lee.12th District of California."https://lee.house.gov.
11. Lee, Barbara. *Renegade for Peace and Justice: Congresswoman Barbara Lee Speaks for Me.* Rowman & Littlefield Publishers, Inc., 2008.
12. "Barbara Lee Family Foundation." https://www.barbaraleefoundation.org.
13. "Knock Down the House Documentary Film." https://knockdownthehouse.com.
14. "Justice Democrats Political Action Committee." https://justicedemocrats.com.
15. "Congresswoman Alexandria Occasio-Cortez." https://ocasiocortez.house.gov.
16. "Congressman Maxwell Alejandro Frost. Central Florida District 10." https://frost.house.gov.
17. "Arena Academy."https://www.arena.run.
18. "Candidate Boot Camp." https://candidatebootcamp.com.
19. "Close the Gap California." https://closethegapca.org.
20. "Emerge America." https://emergeamerica.org.
21. "Run for Something." https://runforsomething.net.

22. "National Democratic Training Committee." https://traindemocrats.org.
23. "Vote, Run, Lead." https://voterunlead.org.
24. "Partners: Run for Something." https://traindemocrats.org.

Chapter 6: Craft Your Message

1. "Martin Luther King, Jr." Nobel Prize. https://www.nobelprize.org/prizes/peace/1964/king/biographical.
2. "Martin Luther King, Jr." NAACP. https://naacp.org/find-resources/history-explained/civil-rights-leaders/martin-luther-king-jr.
3. "March for Our Lives." https://marchforourlives.com.
4. "Fridays for Future." https://fridaysforfuture.org.
5. "Robert Reich." https://robertreich.org.
6. "Colin Kaepernick." https://kaepernick7.com.
7. "Know Your Rights Camp." https://www.knowyourrightscamp.org.
8. "Colin Kaepernick's Change the Whirled Non-Dairy." Ben & Jerry's. https://www.benjerry.com/flavors/colin-kaepernicks-change-the-whirled-non-dairy.
9. "Inequality Media." https://www.inequalitymedia.org.
10. "Ocasio-Cortez campaign design." Vox. https://www.vox.com/policy-and-politics/2018/7/2/17519414/ocasio-cortez-campaign-design-campaign-posters-tandem-branding.
11. "Alexandria Ocasio-Cortez campaign." The Intercept. https://theintercept.com/2019/05/30/alexandria-ocasio-cortez-campaign.
12. "Oregon Food Bank." https://www.oregonfoodbank.org.

Step 3: GO!

1. "Nelson Mandela." https://www.nelsonmandela.org/content/page/biography.
2. "Nelson Mandela, Nobel Peace Prize." https://www.nobelprize.org/prizes/peace/1993/mandela/biographical.

Chapter 7: Organize a Movement

1. "John Lewis." U.S. House of Representatives: History, Art & Archives. https://history.house.gov/People/Detail/16948.

2. Ganz, Marshall. "Organizing: People, Power, Change." Harvard University. https://actionnetwork.org/user_files/user_files/000/041/455/original/organizing_people_power_changeadaptedfromMarshall-Ganz.pdf.
3. Shaw, R. (2013). The Activist's Handbook: Winning Social Change in the 21st Century. University of California Press.
4. "Trans Empowerment Project." https://transempowerment.org.
5. Hellén, K. (2019, November 8). Chalk Dust of the Revolution: Reflections of a Chalkstar. Due Dissidence. https://duedissidence.com/archives/2019/11/08/chalk-dust-of-the-revolution-reflections-of-a-chalkstar.
6. "Democratic Socialists of America." Democratic Socialists of America. https://www.dsausa.org.
7. Nonprofit Technology Enterprise Network (NTEN)." https://www.nten.org.
8. Nonprofit Tech for Good." https://www.nptechforgood.com/
9. "Social Movement Technologies." https://socialmovementtechnologies.org.
10. "Action Network." https://actionnetwork.org.
11. "Nonprofit for Good." https://www.nptechforgood.com.
12. "Hustle." https://hustle.com.
13. "Black Lives Matter." https://blacklivesmatter.com.
14. "We Are Somebody." https://wearesomebody.org.
15. McLaughlin, Gayle. *Winning Richmond: How a Progressive Alliance Won City Hall.* Hardball Press, 2018.
16. "Jovanka Beckles for State Senate." https://jovanka4casenate.com.
17. "Civilian Conservation Corps." History. https://www.history.com/topics/great-depression/civilian-conservation-corps.
18. "Everything You Need to Know About the American Climate Corps." Evergreen Action. https://www.evergreenaction.com/blog/american-climate-corps.
19. "Find Your Representatives." My Reps. https://myreps.datamade.us.
20. "Track Legislation." GovTrack. https://www.govtrack.us.

Chapter 8: Get Out the Vote

1. "Susan B. Anthony." Susan B. Anthony House. https://susanb.org/her-life.

2. "Women's Suffrage Movement." Britannica. https://www.britannica.com/topic/woman-suffrage.
3. Pelosi, Christine. *Campaign Boot Camp. Basic Training for Future Leaders.* PoliPointPress, CA, 2007.
4. Shaw, Catherine. *The Campaign Manager. Running and Winning Local Elections.* Routledge, NY, 2018.
5. "Primary Election Dates." U.S. Vote Foundation. https://www.usvotefoundation.org/primary-election-dates.
6. "I Will Vote." https://iwillvote.com.
7. "Cori Bush." U.S. House of Representatives. https://bush.house.gov.

Chapter 9: Count Every Vote

1. John Wooden, *They Call Me Coach.* NY, McGraw-Hill Books, 2024.
2. "Pyramid of Success." The Wooden Effect. https://www.thewoodeneffect.com/pyramid-of-success.
3. "Coach Wooden." https://coachwooden.com.
4. "U.S. Election Assistance Commission What does a poll worker do? How do I volunteer?" https://www.eac.gov/what-does-a-poll-worker-do.
5. "League of Women Voters." https://www.lwv.org.
6. "Vote 411." https://www.vote411.org.
7. "Kareem Abdul-Jabbar Substack." https://kareem.substack.com/
8. Fricano, M. (2016). Do you know what Kareem Abdul-Jabbar has accomplished since retiring from the NBA? https://newsroom.ucla.edu/stories/do-you-know-what-kareem-abdul-jabbar-has-accomplished-since-retiring.

Acknowledgements

This book is a tribute to the power of collective action. I am deeply grateful to all the campaigns, candidates, and cause organizations that have shared their work, best practices, and learnings. The relentless efforts of those before us, both in the U.S. and around the world, have ignited major changes and movements. Your inspiration, wisdom, and experiences have been invaluable and have added depth and authenticity to this book.

Your dedication is inspiring, and your journeys continue to motivate us all. I am particularly thankful to Bernie Sanders for uniting us to build a movement. This book is not just a product of our collective effort, but a symbol of our unwavering commitment to campaigns, candidates, and causes that strive for safer communities, a healthier planet, and justice for all.

A special shout-out to the Chapter Digital Strategies *Dream Team*. Your collaboration and trust have been invaluable in implementing the 'Ready, Set, Go' process.

Thank you to my partner, Kathy, for your support, patience, and love. To the reviewers of the manuscript and cover design, Dawna Knapp, Kate Kátima Henke, Leslie Armijo, and Kathy Sharp, thank you for your valuable feedback and creativity. You have made the book better.

Last but not least, thank you to my family. Your constant support and encouragement have been my source of strength throughout this journey.

About the Author

Kacey Carpenter is an accomplished author, activist, and community organizer with a rich background in digital innovation.

He has a passion for life, family, friends, and the outdoors, and he loves coaching, teaching, traveling, and volunteering. Kacey's life journey changed when he served as a Bernie Sanders delegate and volunteered extensively—experiences that propelled him to run for city council, become a delegate for the California Democratic Party, and actively support grassroots campaigns, candidates, and causes. His first book, "My Journey with Bernie," chronicles this inspiring journey.

With over three decades of experience, he has worked at the intersection of technology, movement building, and organizations across non-profits, as well as the public and private sectors. He holds an MBA from The Wharton School at the University of Pennsylvania and a Bachelor of Science degree from UCLA.

Kacey lives with his partner Kathy in Oregon. He is an active volunteer leader with the Oregon chapters of the National Writers Union and Sierra Club local outings. He has volunteered for Mexipets Paws Without Borders to rescue 4 dogs and 2 cats from Mexico to new families in California. His service extends beyond these organizations as he passionately supports campaigns, candidates, and causes where he tirelessly works to uphold democracy, safeguard our planet, and advocate for equity, inclusion, and justice for all.

For more information, please join his newsletter "Life is a Journey" at: lifeisajourney.substack.com.

www.ingramcontent.com/pod-product-compliance
Lightning Source LLC
LaVergne TN
LVHW010313070526
838199LV00065B/5543